*The Light Within Me*

# THE LIGHT WITHIN ME

*An Inspirational Memoir*

# AINSLEY EARHARDT

*with Mark Tabb*

HARPER

NEW YORK • LONDON • TORONTO • SYDNEY

## HARPER

All Scripture quotations, unless otherwise indicated, are taken from the Holy Bible, New International Version®, NIV®. Copyright ©1973, 1978, 1984, 2011 by Biblica, Inc.™ Used by permission of Zondervan. All rights reserved worldwide. www.zondervan.com The "NIV" and "New International Version" are trademarks registered in the United States Patent and Trademark Office by Biblica, Inc.™

Photographs, unless otherwise credited, are courtesy of the author.

A hardcover edition of this book was published in 2018 by HarperCollins Publishers.

THE LIGHT WITHIN ME. @ Copyright © 2018, 2020 by Ainsley Earhardt. All rights reserved. Printed in the United States of America. No part of this book may be used or reproduced in any manner whatsoever without written permission except in the case of brief quotations embodied in critical articles and reviews. For information, address HarperCollins Publishers, 195 Broadway, New York, NY 10007.

HarperCollins books may be purchased for educational, business, or sales promotional use. For information, please email the Special Markets Department at SPsales@harpercollins.com.

FIRST HARPER PAPERBACKS EDITION PUBLISHED 2020.

Library of Congress Cataloging-in-Publication Data has been applied for.

ISBN 978-0-06-269748-6 (pbk.)

20 21 22 23 24   LSC   10 9 8 7 6 5 4 3 2 1

*I dedicate this book to my Lord and Savior, Jesus Christ.*

*I no longer fear death because I know*

*I will have eternal life with Christ.*

I have come into the world as a light, so that no one who believes in me should stay in darkness.

JOHN 12:46

# Contents

*The Light Within Me*

# I

## A Firm Foundation

Start children off on the way they should go, and even
when they are old they will not turn from it.

—PROVERBS 22:6

M Y MOM CALLED recently and in the course of our conversation she said, "My friends all tell me they wake up with
you every day. And I thought to myself, *You wake up with my
daughter?* But then it hit me. They were talking about your news
show." And then she added, "Honey, I think you might be famous."

"I know, Mom. It's so crazy." We both laughed at the idea. My
mom wasn't the first to say something like this to me. Not long
after my daughter was born I was talking to a group of girlfriends
about schools and I expressed my apprehension about getting
Hayden into the right one. "Oh, you won't have a problem," one
said. "You're a daytime news anchor."

"Yes, but I don't feel that makes any difference," I replied.

They all tried to set me straight. "Ainsley, you have to see yourself the way others see you."

I don't think that's right. I may have a very visible job that
allows more than a million viewers to invite me and my fellow
anchors into their homes every morning, but that doesn't make
me famous; nor does my job entitle me to any kind of special priv-
ileges. When I think of the position that's been entrusted to me, I
feel a great weight of responsibility. Not a day goes by that I don't
look at myself in the mirror and ask God, "Why me? Why did
you choose me, Ainsley Earhardt from Columbia, South Carolina,

to be one of a handful of female national news anchors?" I don't know the complete answer to this question except to say that God put me here for a reason and that reason has nothing to do with me becoming famous.

Now, I have to admit that I didn't always feel this way. When I was five years old I remember watching the opening of the Oscars with my mother and crying as I watched celebrities walk in on the red carpet. Why would any child cry watching the Oscars? For me, the reason was simple: I wanted to be there so badly that I burst into tears. I remember telling my mother that someday I was going to live in California and be a famous actress.

"California," my mother replied, "life's a beach there."

I had no idea what that meant.

Around the same time, my siblings and I were looked after by a wonderful lady named Miriam "Mimi" Grant until my mom got home from work. Every day when she put us down for our naps, she turned on the television to watch her soap operas. I knew about soaps because my great-grandmother called them "the stories" and always told my mother they were sinful. My great-grandmother's warning didn't stop me from sneaking out of my bed and tiptoeing into the den behind our babysitter where she couldn't see me and watching them. The actors were all beautiful and seemed to have perfect lives. The entire idea of being in front of the camera seemed so romantic. Deep down I just knew that that would be me someday, either in front of a camera or on the stage. My parents indulged my fantasies, to a point. I attended theater camps and classes growing up, but there was never any talk of me making a life out of acting. My parents were much too practical and grounded for that.

I actually got my chance to be in the movies while I was still in middle school. Twice. The first time occurred when Disney came to South Carolina to shoot a movie set in the 1930s called

*Wild Hearts Can't Be Broken.* As soon as I heard they needed extras I was determined to land a part. I went to the auditions and was selected to be one of the kids in the crowd when the female star's love interest, Michael Schoeffling, was getting into an argument with a group of men at the local fair. Years before, he had been the actor in *Sixteen Candles* who kissed Molly Ringwald at the end of the movie and was just so handsome to me at the time.

Actually being chosen to be a child in the crowd made my little middle school heart race. I just knew that this was going to be my big break and one of the directors was going to notice me. And they did. They needed a girl for a larger part than just a face in the crowd, and this role would actually get a line or two. One of the directors pulled me out of the crowd of extras along with another girl. I was thrilled—this was my chance. But then I gave them a big smile and they saw the braces on my teeth.

"She can't do it," they said. "Braces don't fit the time period."

I was heartbroken. Instead of a speaking part I ended up in the background wearing a red dress and eating cotton candy.

My second time came in a movie about college football called *The Program*. This one starred Halle Berry and James Caan. The movie auditions and information made the local news because it was filmed in my hometown and scenes were shot at the University of South Carolina's Williams-Brice Stadium. Since this movie was set in the present, my braces weren't a problem. I went to the auditions with a head full of dreams. However, once again, I was just a face in the crowd in a background filled with extras.

My middle school girl visions of fame did not come true, but they also did not die—and thankfully my mom and dad knew just the right approach to raising a daughter with dreams of grandeur. My mom used to tease me, saying she hoped I married a rich man someday because I was such a dreamer with champagne taste.

She didn't mean that the way it sounds. It was her way of telling me to get my head out of the clouds. Dreams don't come true by waiting for Prince Charming to arrive. If my dreams were going to come true it was going to be because of my own hard work.

My mother showed me the power of hard work and determination. She taught early childhood development, but she was no ordinary teacher. I watched my mother go through the very rigorous process of becoming a national board-certified teacher. Only 3 percent of all teachers across America are nationally board certified. The process is so demanding that only 40 percent of those who attempt it make it through the first year. But my mom completed the program while working full-time, raising three kids, and running our household. Watching her taught me that hard work, not dreams of grandeur, is the key to success in life.

My father taught me confidence, which allowed me to follow my dreams and never be afraid of rejection. When I was a little girl my dad coached basketball at Wofford College in Spartanburg, South Carolina. He also had big goals of moving up the coaching ladder from Wofford and becoming the head coach of a major college program. His real dream job was at his alma mater, the University of South Carolina. However, one year after my little brother was born my dad left coaching and took a job selling janitorial and industrial supplies. We moved from Spartanburg to Charlotte, North Carolina. I completed my third grade year at Sharon Elementary School (which I would later learn was the same school two other Fox News anchors attended), but after that school year, my father's company had an open position in his hometown of Columbia, South Carolina. We all missed South Carolina and were delighted to pack up and move again. Instantly, my father was successful. He proved himself to be one of the top salespeople in his company. It wasn't just that he was a good salesman—he worked incredibly hard and was very well-liked. I can still see him sitting up late at night writing out thank-you notes to all the customers he saw that day.

As my older sister, Elise, my brother, Trent, and I got older and closer to college age, my dad worked side jobs. Sometimes that meant cleaning floors for businesses at night or delivering the loads of toilet paper a company needed for the following morning. He was also in the Army Reserves. He served at Fort Jackson one weekend every month and two weeks every summer. He sacrificed a lot for our family and hard work was celebrated and expected in our home. He did all of this because he had a second dream, the dream of putting all three of his children through college. Growing up, I never saw Dad use a credit card, he paid with cash and I remember him telling me he made double payments toward the mortgage every month until it was paid off. He believed in working hard now so you can enjoy the fruits of your labor later.

The value of hard work was only one small lesson my parents taught me. For the first few years of my life, we lived in a one-story, L-shaped house in Spartanburg with a huge backyard with many colorful azalea bushes and honeysuckles, a gorgeous dogwood tree in the front yard, and a massive magnolia tree which separated us from our neighbors. Elise moved into my bedroom with me when our brother was born. I was five and a half when he came along, and I was very excited about having a baby to love. Elise and I fought over who got to feed him, change his diapers, and take care of him. On his wedding day we joked that he'd been raised with three moms. Poor guy. We couldn't help ourselves. Having a baby brother was like having a real, live baby doll.

Because of her teaching job, my mom always left the house early, which left my dad to get us up and ready for school. He'd come into our room and wake us up by opening the shutters and sometimes tickling us. There was no sleeping in at the Earhardt house, not even on the weekends. Saturday mornings he came in early, threw open the shutters, and said, "Rise and shine. It's time to get up. If I'm up, you're up!" We'd drag ourselves out of bed and go downstairs for breakfast.

Most mornings I found a little note next to my cereal bowl in which my dad had written out a quote or a Bible verse or a poem he'd found. Since he was a great coach, I imagine these were the same kinds of sayings he used to motivate his players. They motivated me. I still have a lot of them today. One of my favorites was, according to my dad, uttered by Walt Disney. It read, "I hope I'll never be afraid to fail." That's how my dad taught me to approach life. I also loved the one that said, "Attitude determines aptitude," and another that said, "Stay up with the owls—don't expect to soar with the eagles." When I got a little older he gave me one that said, "Nothing good happens after midnight."

I loved these notes. I did not, however, love his habit of making us drink a glass of unsweetened grapefruit juice every morning. My sister and brother and I held our noses as we forced it down. Apparently my dad had read somewhere that grapefruit juice helped prevent sickness.

After breakfast we piled into the car for the car pool to school. My favorite days were those when my dad brought home the team van from the college where he coached. Elise and I would cheer when he would drive it home the night before and we saw it parked in front of our house or in the driveway. On car-pool days one of us always hid behind the backseat while my dad picked up the other kids. They climbed in the van and asked, "Where's Elise?" or "Where's Ainsley?" We said something like "Oh, she stayed home sick today," which of course never happened because of all the grapefruit juice we drank. Then, once everyone was in the van, whoever was hiding in the back jumped out and yelled, "SURPRISE!" Elise and I thought that was great. The joke never got old.

Whether we were in the van or not, my dad always made the drive to school interesting. Every day we drove past a big tree with a hole in the middle of it. My dad told us a bear lived in the hole. He even had a name for the bear. Another house on our route had a large clubhouse in the backyard that looked like a dollhouse. Whenever we passed by it my dad said, "You know, the Smurfs live in that dollhouse. I wonder if they're awake. Let's honk the horn and wake 'em up." We always laughed.

Mom was still at work when we got home from school. Mimi took care of us when we were very young in Spartanburg, South Carolina, but when we moved to Columbia, I was in fourth grade and Elise was in seventh. By that point, we were old enough to come home to an empty house, make a snack, and watch TV until Mom came home. Elise and I would watch a soap opera called *Santa Barbara*, which is no longer on the air, but when we heard Mom opening the garage door, we had to quickly turn off the TV, since we still were not allowed to watch soaps. We'd run upstairs to our bedrooms and start working on our homework. My brother was usually outside playing with all the boys in the neighborhood. Mom started dinner along with doing everything else that had to be done to keep the household running. My sister, brother, and I did our part. All of us had daily chores. Now that I am a mother I have a newfound respect for my mom. Honestly, I don't know how she did it. I find it is hard enough to be a working mom with only one child . . . somehow she did it with three.

GROWING UP, WE talked about God in our home and said a blessing at every meal and prayers before bed. I definitely grew up in a Christian environment, but we didn't read the Bible as a family every night or memorize Scripture. Instead my parents would find their own ways to remind me of God's place in my life, which gave me a good perspective on life and the disappointments it brings.

When I was in eighth grade I tried out for the cheerleading squad. I thought it was going to be an easy audition because I had been on the squad the previous year and got along beautifully with the coach and other cheerleaders. However, when the list of girls who made the team was posted, my name was missing. I was crushed. Six of the current cheerleaders in seventh grade didn't make the team for the next year. We were all in tears and being consoled by our coach who was also emotional. She cried with us. When I got home and shared the news with my parents, my dad said something I have never forgotten. "You got to be a cheerleader last year, right?" he said.

"Yes, sir."

"Another girl probably needed that spot this year more than you. Ainsley, God knew you could handle the rejection of not making the squad. He made you a confident, positive person. You will be fine. He will bless you in other ways, just wait and see," he said. Those words have stuck with me the rest of my life. My dad taught me to look at life's setbacks through eyes of faith.

We attended church every Sunday. Church on Sundays was a must—even if we spent the night with a friend. We either went with the friend or Mom and Dad picked us up early from the friend's house and we went to our own church as a family. When we lived in Spartanburg and Charlotte, we attended very formal Episcopal churches. They were beautiful, with stained-glass windows, long aisles, and sanctuaries shaped like a cross that are traditional for Episcopal churches. When we moved to Columbia, my father felt very strongly about joining Ebenezer Lutheran Church. That was the church he grew up in and generations of our Earhardt relatives had attended services there. It was a relatively long drive for us, about fifteen or twenty minutes, but Dad felt God calling him back to his childhood church. The members of the congregation were older and there weren't a lot of young families. Dad knew God wanted him to help grow the church and bring new life into an older congregation, so the whole family got involved. My dad served on the church council and my mom was part of the altar guild. In high school I represented the youth group on the church council and became youth-group president. This was also the church where I was confirmed.

Church was a big part of my life growing up, but something still seemed to be missing. Every year our church youth group attended Lutheran Christian camps as well as taking ski trips and other activities. I was confirmed and very active, but I still felt like something was missing. This wasn't enough. I remember one day riding to high school with one of my best friends, Cindy, and asking her a question that was heavy on my heart.

"Cindy, how do you know you're going to heaven?" I asked.

"Well, if you are a good person, you will go to heaven," she said.

"I feel like I am a good person and I try to be nice to everyone, but I don't know if that's going to get me to heaven," I replied. Deep down I knew that it wasn't enough. I wanted to be certain. Then I reminded myself that I was not worthy of heaven and, of course, I never expected God to think I was good enough. I remember thinking I was only allowed a few prayers; God would think I was selfish if I had too many requests. I knew He was busy answering prayers all over the world, so I told myself I could only talk to God when the prayer was selfless or really important. I thought of it as "saving my favors for when I really needed a prayer answered." Therefore, I decided to try my hardest to get to heaven and hope for the best when I came face-to-face with Him at the Pearly Gates.

Going to church and trying to be a good person didn't keep me from doing things that deep down I knew I shouldn't do. My friends and I always wanted to be in the middle of the fun, so when we heard about a party, we were there. Through high school and my first two years of college I did things that were considered normal for people my age. For instance, most of my friends were smokers. At that time students were allowed to smoke at my high school. We were born in the seventies and most high schoolers took part. In fact, we even had a designated smoking area at school called "The Back Porch." Occasionally I walked out and took a few drags of a friend's cigarette. Smoking was a social event for me. It was just something most people did. We all hid it from our parents, but truth be told, many of them smoked, too, so we picked up the habit. We knew it was not healthy, but all my friends just assumed we could smoke through high school and college, hide it from our parents, and then quit when we got married one day.

It was pretty naive, especially considering I'd witnessed first-hand how hard it was to quit the nicotine habit. My mother smoked when I was little. My dad, sister, and I HATED it. My mother's parents, my Mimi and Pop, smoked. They smoked inside their house and in their cars. The smell was awful. Still, to this day, when I get in the car of a smoker, it takes me back to my childhood and makes my stomach turn. But Mimi, Pop, Mom, and her sister, Lynn, all gave up the habit together when Pop was diagnosed with a lung disease. It was not easy for Mom. She quit for ten years, but started smoking again later and tried hiding it from all of us. Dad has never smoked. He is our practical thinker. So Mom hid her smoking from him. We all did. If he had known I was a smoker, he would have been extremely disappointed. One time he discovered a pack of my cigarettes on the front walkway outside, and I later found them on my pillowcase. That was his way of saying, "I don't want a confrontation or hear you try to lie your way out of it, but I want you to know how deeply disappointed I am." That hurt. I knew I had let him down.

When I started smoking more and more throughout high school, I decided if I was going to pick up this nasty habit, I was going to do it in the most glamorous way. After all, my friends already called me "Hollywood." So I bought a silver cigarette case and filled it with my cigarette of choice: the skinny, minty Virginia Slim Super Slim menthol. We shortened the name to the "VSSS." When my friends wanted one, they said, "Hollywood, may I have one of your VSSS's?" I smiled and handed them my cigarette case—enjoying every minute of it.

I didn't think anything I did was that inconsistent with attending church on Sundays. The Lutheran Church didn't cast condemnation or make me feel guilty. I knew my parents and God wouldn't approve of my choices, but I was still able to separate my social and church lives. It was as though those two parts of my life stayed in their own spheres. As I got older and was able to go out at night (my curfew was 11 P.M.), we all lied to our parents, went to parties on Saturday nights, and then showed up bright and early for church on Sunday mornings. That didn't seem like a big deal. Everyone else did the same thing. In fact, most of the time I felt pretty good about my life. I had a Bible, actually several. My dad gave them to me. I kept one of them next to my bed, and I read Scripture when I was sad or going through a tough time. My best friend Cindy, who drove me to school, gave me a bookmark with Scripture verses that correlated to particular emotions.

And yet, when I was around people who were really "sold out" for Jesus, I knew something was missing in my life. One guy, Eric, in particular really made an impression on me. He hung out with the most popular people and was quite outspoken about his faith. He was older than I was and had a long-term relationship with a girl in Atlanta. He told everybody they were committed to wait until marriage before having sex. That made an impression on me. I wanted to be that kind of person as well. Around the same time, our youth group leader played a Christian video for us talking about sex and the struggles high school students experience. One girl in the video said, "I am still a virgin, and any day I can be like my friends, but they can never go back and be like me." Although I know now God is all about redemption and grace, I still wanted my virginity to be a special gift I gave my husband on our wedding night. That was important to me.

Eric was the closest thing on earth to Jesus for me. Somehow he was able to live a solid, Christian life, make good choices, and surround himself with the smokers and drinkers. As John 17:16 suggests, he was in the world but not of the world. I wanted to be like that. So, when he hosted Young Life, a campus ministry geared toward high school students, at his parents' house—I was there. There was always pizza, good snacks, Coca-Colas, and a good mix of the social crowd and Christian crowd. I always wanted to go and never wanted to leave.

We all congregated in Eric's basement and sat on the carpet in front of a movie screen that displayed the words of contemporary Christian songs. One leader played the guitar and another sang. After we sang a mix of secular and Christian songs, one of the Young Life leaders told his or her story or gave a Bible lesson. One college leader, who was cute and seemed cool (all of the high school girls loved him), shared his story about Jesus saving him from a life of alcohol and drugs. Although I had no desire to do drugs, I was still taken aback. This guy's story seemed much more dramatic than just going to confirmation classes.

I also had someone in my life, even to this day I have no idea who, that put letters in my mailbox at random times. When the first one arrived I opened it and read, "This is Jesus. I just wanted to tell you that I love you." Another said, "I watched you go through your day today. You were so busy but you never made time for me. Love, Jesus." I still have many of those letters today.

In spite of the letters, and the testimonies at Young Life, the only dramatic decision I made about my life during high school was to go to college. I knew something was missing in my life, but I also had a strong sense that God had something in store for me that was bigger than high school, my hometown, and even South Carolina. I didn't crave fame, like I had when I was a little girl, but I was still in love with the idea of becoming an actress. As high school drew to a close I really wanted to attend a college with a great theater program, but I knew my parents would never go for it. My dad wasn't working multiple jobs for me to major in something that had such an uncertain future. Whatever I did, I wanted to repay my parents' efforts by working hard, to give back to them for all they'd done for me.

# 2

# At a Crossroads

Trust in the Lord with all your heart and lean not on
your own understanding; in all your ways submit to
him, and he will make your paths straight.

—PROVERBS 3:5–6

I MAY HAVE grown up dreaming of becoming an actress, but by
the time I went off to college, I was convinced I should become
an orthodontist. While it seems odd today to think of myself doing
anything other than broadcast journalism, my family orthodontist convinced me that I should follow in his footsteps.

Dr. Richard Boyd was not only my orthodontist but a family friend, a mentor, and a Godsend. When he put the first set of
braces on my teeth I was twelve years old and quite excited. Every
middle school student wanted crooked teeth—just so they could
be Dr. Boyd's patient. One waiting room in his office was set up
like a big playroom for kids, with all the latest toys and gadgets,
including a Sega Genesis system, which was huge at the time. On
the parents' side of the office he offered free drinks from a mini–
soda machine along with coffee, hot chocolate, cider, and fresh
baked cookies. A big bulletin board covered one wall with photos
of all the kids who'd gotten their braces off. Every time I went
in I studied the board to see if any of my friends were on it, or if
there were any cute, older boys from my school. Needless to say,
everyone I knew with braces went to Dr. Boyd. The treatment
room was set up with all the typical dentist chairs in one big area
rather than being separated into individual cubicles. That allowed

my friends and me to talk while we waited our turns to have our braces adjusted. At the end of the appointment, when it was time to schedule my next visit, the front-desk ladies always asked me if I wanted to make it for a time when my friends were in the office too. Dr. Boyd and his staff actually made having braces fun.

One summer night right before the start of my freshman year of high school Dr. Boyd and his wife, Stacy, came over to our house. When they were leaving, my entire family went out on the porch with them to tell them good-bye. It was a hot summer night with lightning bugs flying around. Dr. Boyd turned to me and asked, "Do you think you would ever want to come work for me?" I couldn't believe my ears. All the girls on his office staff wore the best, matching clothes from the coolest stores. I think my first question was, "Do I get the clothes too?" He agreed and also threw in a few extra perks, including good hourly pay and a chance to go on the annual office work trip. Dr. Boyd usually took the staff to the national convention for orthodontists and gave us a few days to explore the city where it was held. My senior year of high school we went to San Francisco. Dr. Boyd was scheduled to speak at the University of the Pacific and he took me to listen to his lecture. I fell in love with California and became very excited about my future. I knew the sky was the limit and the choices I made at that point would direct my path and determine my life's trajectory.

Over the next four years of high school I rotated jobs at Dr. Boyd's office. The first year I worked in the back bay, where we saw the patients. I sterilized instruments, helped with molds for the retainers, and made up the bags filled with all the candy we couldn't eat while we were wearing braces; Dr. Boyd gave them to his patients when he took off their braces. Later I worked the front desk, making appointments. When I got my driver's license I ran errands for the office and for the Boyd family. Eventually he let me look inside the patients' mouths, with their parents' permission, and he showed me how to change the "ties," that is, the bands around each bracket. When the young, middle school girls asked me if they should get ties in different colors, I always said yes. I encouraged them to be themselves and choose fun colors that evoked their personalities or a certain holiday.

Since I was a high school girl working in the office, the middle school girls looked up to me. That gave me such a heart for young girls which I carry still to this day. Middle school is a time when girls first shave their legs, get their ears pierced, and get their first bra. It is a meaningful time for a girl. You are growing up and becoming a woman. As an employee at Dr. Boyd's office, I felt privileged to have a small influence on these young, precious girls. Plus, I enjoyed working. I liked having a schedule and loved getting a paycheck. I was able to pay for my own clothes, gas, food, and even my senior trip. I took great pride in telling friends I had to go to work (instead of hanging out after class) and telling my dad I did not need lunch money when he'd ask me each day. Looking back, I think he took great pride himself in not giving me the five-dollar bill. He had the money, but knew taking care of myself was a good lesson for me to learn.

As I have said, Dad and Mom worked hard to save money for my sister, brother, and me to go to college. They are good people and parents. They wanted to give us nice lives while also teaching us the value of a dollar and the importance of hard work. Knowing that, I always enjoyed paying my own way. I wanted to relieve my parents' stress and help them out however I could. Dr. Boyd gave me a great opportunity. He was flexible about my schedule, gave me hours Monday through Friday, and understood if I had a school commitment and couldn't come to work. By the time I was ready to go off to college, he told me if I became an orthodontist, I could take over his practice eventually. He even offered to help with the cost of dental school after college. With that said, he knew I wanted to be an actress and that Mom and Dad were never going to let me major in theater. While I had not given up on my dream of living in California or New York, I was also realistic. I loved my high school science classes, and Dr. Boyd made such a great offer that I decided to major in biology then go on to dental school to become an orthodontist.

I applied to six colleges and narrowed down my choices to Clemson University, which was a couple of hours from home in northwest South Carolina, and Florida State University, which was more than six hours away in Tallahassee. My parents told us we had to go to an in-state school unless we had a scholarship that made the cost the same as in-state tuition. I was up for a scholarship at Florida State, but despite calling every day, I had not heard anything definitive and it was time to make my choice. On deadline day my friend Jamie and I drove to Clemson to turn in nonrefundable checks. We had to pay that first check or lose our spots. However, before I handed my check over I called the admissions office at FSU one last time. The woman on the other end of the phone did some checking; when she came back to me, she said, "Ainsley, you got the scholarship!" This was ordained.

Her words were the answer to my prayers. I couldn't believe the impeccable timing. After I heard the news I thanked God then called my parents. I knew God was in this. He kept me on my knees the entire time—all the way until the end—only to bless me at the last moment. My friend Jamie handed over her check with pure excitement. Her entire family had graduated from Clemson and this was her dream come true. Meanwhile, I took my check home and gave it back to my dad. The Florida State scholarship covered about half of the cost of tuition, which made it about the same price as a state school in South Carolina. God's timing is perfect. Everything worked out and I was Florida bound.

I DOVE INTO college life. Just like high school, I was always the good girl, but if fun was going on, I wanted to be in the middle of it. My classes were hard, especially chemistry. I didn't help myself much by staying out late and trying to cram in some study time in the middle of the night. I also had a part-time job. Dr. Boyd arranged for me to work for an orthodontist in Tallahassee, which provided more experience, training, and spending money.

The first big decision I had to make when I moved into my dorm was which sorority I should rush. While that may seem like an insignificant decision, it actually proved to be life-changing. At Florida State you have to visit all sixteen sororities before choosing one. The Greek Council gives you a schedule, you visit the sorority houses, and meet hundreds of young women. I remember my mouth killing me from the plastered smile I wore for a week. I was torn between Pi Beta Phi and Alpha Delta Pi. I called my mom and said, "This is the biggest decision I've ever made in my life. Which sorority should I choose?" We still laugh about that to this day, but, at the time, it was important to me. By the end of rush I knew. I wanted Alpha Delta Pi. I can honestly say, God helped me make that decision. He saw the future and knew how this decision would change the course of my life.

BETWEEN CLASSES AND work I was too busy to get homesick. Tallahassee is four hundred and fifty miles from my parents' house. Although I love my mom and dad, being that far away taught me independence. Going to a big school did not intimidate me. I was ready to be on my own.

As someone who's always up for adventure, I am definitely my father's child, but I also have a lot of my mom in me. She appreciates art, museums, and travel. She grew up in a country club environment and has an understanding of the finer things in life. My proper, maternal grandparents were members of a long-standing, traditional debutante club in Greenville called The Carolinian. My mother and her sister, Aunt Lynn, made their debuts their sophomore years in college and my sister and I were expected to do the same. We really didn't have a choice, but it turned out to be a great experience. I met some lifelong friends, and it pleased my grandparents and mother.

The parties begin the summer before your sophomore year— and anyone who throws you a party gets an invitation to the big ball in December. So there were many parties in honor of the debutantes. There were lunches during the day, tennis matches at the Greenville Country Club in the afternoon and elaborate, themed parties at night. I was busy and decided to just live with my Mimi and Pop for the summer. My parents lived two hours away. When the summer was over, I went back to Tallahassee for my sophomore year and made my debut that Christmas in Green-ville. One of the debutantes, Eden, was a devout Christian and we became good friends. I admired her for the way she lived her life. She was kind, never missed church on Sunday mornings, and went on mission trips with her church. Her college friends at Wake Forest University were strong Christians, too. She was different from most college kids and so were her friends. The morning after we made our debuts, I went to Eden's hotel room (we were all staying at a big hotel downtown together) to talk to her about the night before, and found her, along with all of her friends, getting ready for church. The whole scene was impressive and I gained even more respect for her. I wanted a group of friends like that too. God was their priority.

ABOUT HALFWAY THROUGH my sophomore year I saw an an-nouncement that Campus Crusade, an on-campus ministry, planned to take a group to New York during spring break for ministry in homeless shelters in New York City. To be honest it didn't matter what the group was. When I saw a chance to go to New York City, I was all over it. One of my friends also signed up, which made me feel relieved because I didn't know anyone in Campus Crusade and I knew my parents would be worried about me going to Manhattan. But then my friend backed out at the last minute, which meant I was going to be with a group of people I did not know, people who were really into Jesus, while all my friends went to Mexico and wherever else on great vacations. Somehow, though, I didn't dread it as much as it might sound. I really, really wanted to go to New York. As for not knowing anyone on the trip, I love meeting new people.

There was also something about this trip that felt like God wanted me to go. Throughout this time in my life I felt God pulling me toward Him. He was pulling and I kept resisting. I thought I'd have to give everything up if I surrendered my life to God. At the same time I saw something in the truly committed Christians that I didn't see in myself, and I wanted it. I wished I could live the way they lived, but wasn't sure how. They were all such good people. They believed they were on this earth to tell others about Christ, and they wanted to be living, breathing examples of how He lived life on Earth. They felt they were called to serve others and make this world see the goodness and glory of Christ. They didn't pretend to be perfect. They were honest with me about their own hardships and struggles. Some had dated people who didn't have their best interests in mind, or came from broken or abusive homes or had backgrounds of drugs or alcohol. Others grew up in the church with parents who were in the ministry. They each had different stories, but the common thread was their love for the Lord and others.

When I boarded the bus for New York all the students made

me feel very welcome, and by the time we arrived I'd become acquainted with most everyone. However, as soon as I stepped off the bus, I was pushed out of my comfort zone. One leader handed me a stack of "tracts" explaining that these would be used to minister to those who were not Christians.

"What the heck is a tract?" I asked. I had never seen tracts before. I didn't know what they were.

"This is how you tell people about Jesus," I was told. They were little, rectangular pamphlets, just a few pages, written in clear, simple language about how to know Jesus. They were designed to help seekers understand who Jesus is, what he had done (died on the cross), and how to have a committed life with Jesus. It was basically a step-by-step guide to becoming a Christian. After you read the little tract to the person you were sharing Christ with, you'd ask them to pray with you. It's called the salvation prayer. Christians believe when you ask Jesus into your life, you get "saved." That means you are saved from hell and are assured you will spend eternity in heaven. The whole idea of going up to random people and telling them about Jesus seemed bizarre to me. Even though my family went to church and we considered ourselves Christians, we were taught that your faith was extremely private. We didn't really talk about it around the dining room table, much less strike up a conversation with a stranger on the subject. But that's what I was supposed to do on this trip. The whole experience made me very uncomfortable and made me wish I'd backed out with my friend. I thought about my friends staying in luxury hotels, visiting tropical islands, and having a blast while I slept on a church floor in Queens visiting homeless shelters with complete strangers. At the same time I enjoyed the sermons, prayers, and music, as well as feeding the homeless in New York, hearing their stories, and trying to help them. Many of them had AIDS and didn't have the money to pay for their medications. I knew they might not have long to live and knew the importance of sharing the love and healing of Jesus. I did wonder, at times during the trip, *What have I gotten myself into?*

As the week progressed I became more comfortable, not so much with the tracts, but with helping people. We went out on the streets of New York and fed the homeless. I heard the saddest stories from many who had lived on the streets their entire lives. Some had lost everything—homes, spouses, children, jobs, money—because of addictions. The entire experience was so humbling. I realized there were hurting people everywhere. My heart broke for them. I came to New York City to help change others, but they opened my eyes and helped change me.

We didn't have a lot of free time during this trip, but I was determined to do something I'd always wanted to do. One of my favorite parts of the morning news shows was seeing the people who stood outside the studios and sometimes got on camera. Since I was in New York, and I didn't know if I'd ever make it back, I figured this was my chance. One morning I got up around three and left for the *Today* show. A few of the other girls came with me. We walked to a subway stop in Queens, jumped on a train, and somehow found our way into midtown Manhattan. We arrived early at the *Today* show and parked ourselves next to the railing. The night before I bought a pink poster board and a Magic Marker and made a sign. People with signs always seemed to get noticed before those without.

Once the show started I waited for my chance. Several times Al Roker stepped outside to meet the crowd and report on the weather. When he came close to me and my friends I held up my poster board sign and jumped up and down. My sign worked! I made it on camera. Back home in South Carolina my parents' phone blew up. One of my cousins out in Washington recorded the show for us since it runs on a three-hour delay out there.

Getting on camera on *Today* was fun, but I had a bigger reason for going to the show and holding up my bright pink sign. Even though I was a biology major who planned on going to dental school, I was already starting to have doubts about this career path. When I went to the *Today* show I didn't just want the cameras to notice me. Deep down I hoped someone with the show might notice me and offer me an internship. They didn't, but the experience gave me a great story.

In the end, the mission trip to New York was not the start of my television career, but after I returned to school, I did begin to question my future. I felt God urging me to get serious about my life and career. By the end of my sophomore year, my unease centered on my decision to major in biology. I had loved my science courses in high school, but the college chemistry classes were ridiculously tough. I had already passed Chem 1 and Chem 2, which meant Organic Chemistry was next. In school, my fellow students always talked about how hard Organic was. As time went on, I started to realize orthodontics wasn't what I wanted to do with my life, which made the classes even harder. It's not easy to excel in something you don't care that much about. When I told Dr. Boyd about my hesitancy he reassured me, saying, "Ainsley, I know you can do this. It will provide you with a great life. The biggest emergency you're ever going to face is a broken bracket or a call about a wire poking a patient in the back of the mouth. You rarely work weekends and you will do really well. And I'll help cover the cost of dental school."

Dr. Boyd's reassurances worked for a while but my growing sense that I wanted to do something else just wouldn't go away. By this point, I knew acting was not an option. I had to find a major that fit my personality. I spoke to girls in my sorority who I admired and had similar interests and time-and-time again I kept hearing the allure of public relations as a career. I hated the thought of telling my parents I was going to change majors because all of my life my father preached "Earhardts never quit." I heard that for the first time in fourth grade when I was the only girl on my soccer team and I was not a good player. All the boys made fun of me and I desperately wanted to quit the team. My dad wouldn't let me. He never let any of us quit anything and now I wanted to quit my major that came with a built-in, sure-thing career. Knowing my parents would never let me do something so drastic, I put my head down and trudged ahead. For a while.

Finally I knew I had to make a change. I was struggling through my classes and didn't want to go on that way for the rest of college and then dental school. At the same time, in my heart, I felt this draw to public relations

One day my sister, Elise, called me and told me to turn on my television. She said Leeza Gibbons was being interviewed about growing up in South Carolina and was talking about how she landed her own talk show and about her experience at the University of South Carolina. She spoke highly of the journalism school and this sparked my interest further. Leeza was one of my role models. She was always active in our community and did a lot of work for juvenile diabetes. My mom has type 1 diabetes and Leeza's niece (who lives in my hometown) does too. So when Leeza spoke . . . I listened. I admired her and wanted to follow a similar career path to hers.

I immediately started talking to people in my community who had connections to the journalism school at South Carolina. When I was in middle school, Martha Fowler hired me at South Carolina Educational Television to anchor a weekly newscast, which aired in schools around the state. I stayed in touch with Martha and saw her at church on Sundays. I approached her about the journalism school, explaining my interest in public relations, and she set up an appointment with one of her friends who was a public-relations professor at the university. I met with that professor and immediately knew this was where I was supposed to be. However, I was hesitant. Transferring to another college meant losing credits and delaying graduation. Plus, I had developed many lasting friendships at FSU, and there was also a great PR school there.

And yet a part of me was excited to start over again and make new friends at USC. Going to school in Columbia meant being closer to home and being surrounded by many people I had known my entire life. Plus, the University of South Carolina was a part of our family identity. My dad and uncle had gone there and I grew up going to most of the football games with my parents or grandparents. My mom's parents were graduates of South Carolina too and actually met on the Horseshoe, a green space on campus. The South Carolina Gamecocks were in my blood.

I didn't know what to do. Rather than worry over the decision I prayed and gave it to God. I told Him that I would do my part and apply to both journalism schools and leave the rest up to Him. I turned in applications to the journalism school at FSU and at USC and waited.

The easiest part of being a Christian is that when you give something to God, you have to trust He will make your path straight. He did that in this situation by making the decision for me. I never anticipated being rejected from the journalism school at FSU. After all, I was a biology major with good grades. Compared to biology, journalism was not the most challenging of majors. I had felt like the whole application process was little more than a formality. Imagine my surprise when I received a rejection letter. I could not believe my eyes. I called the admissions office and asked them why.

"You didn't fill out the application correctly," the woman on the other end of the line said. "You did not check off the box declaring the field in which you wanted to major."

All I could think when she said that was, *Wow. That does not sound like me at all.* I am meticulous with everything I do. I make sure every *i* is dotted and every *t* is crossed and every box declaring a specific area of major is checked off. Then I heard from South Carolina telling me that I'd been accepted. Now my decision was a no-brainer. In the words of Yogi Berra, "When you come to a fork in the road, take it." So that's what I did.

First though, I had to tell my parents. I thought they would be disappointed in me for wanting a change. After all, the Earhardt kids were notorious for trying something—tennis, softball, soccer—and then not wanting to continue. But, when I finally got up the courage to talk to my mom about my decision she surprised me.

"Ainsley, you should try it," she said. "If you don't like it you can always go back." That was what I needed to hear.

While this may sound like transferring was easy, it wasn't. Even after the rejection letter from FSU I wondered if I was making the right decision. But having my parents' support made the decision a little easier. Mom was right: if I didn't like USC I could always go back to FSU. The parents who never let me quit anything were now allowing me to grow up on my own. They were teaching me a valuable lesson by letting me live my life. I got to choose now. They basically told me: You are an adult and you can always change your course if you are unhappy. It's a lesson I wrote about in my first children's book and something I will always teach my own daughter. My father says you only have one life. This is not a dress rehearsal. Follow your heart and the Lord will guide you.

When I agonized over the decision of whether or not to transfer, God took the pressure off me and made the choice for me. At the time I thought the decision was purely about my major and my future career. Little did I know that God had other plans.

# 3

## *Meeting Jesus at a Frat Party*

Therefore, if anyone is in Christ, the new creation has
come: The old has gone, the new is here!

—2 CORINTHIANS 5:17

Nᴏᴛ ʟᴏɴɢ ᴀꜰᴛᴇʀ I started at Fox News I went down to Panama City, Florida, to report on what really goes on during
spring break on the beach. I expected to find a lot of kids just having fun, but what I saw shocked me. Maybe it was because I saw
it through the eyes of a thirtysomething reporter who'd recently
landed her dream job, but my heart broke for the girls I interviewed. Whenever our cameras showed up, girls started flashing
us and doing crazy stuff for attention. I also interviewed several
girls who'd been arrested for underage drinking. One girl, I will
never forget, begged me not to put her face on television because
her grandmother watched Fox News.

It was a hard story to report, mostly because I knew how few
of them were considering the consequences of their actions. I made
my share of mistakes along the way, but back then we didn't have
to worry about cell-phone pictures or social media. The kids growing up now will always be haunted by the mistakes they made
years before because now everything is so public.

My first two years at FSU were about fun. I didn't think nearly
as much as I should have about my future or being serious about
school. Even though I was taking some really difficult chemistry
and biology classes, I always found the time for friends and parties. But, as the end of my second year approached, I knew it was

time to start thinking about what I really wanted to do with my life and get serious about pursuing it. That's why I changed majors and it is why I transferred back to my hometown of Columbia and the University of South Carolina. When I first went away to school more than six hours from home, I wanted to be able to stretch my own wings. Now I was ready to get back to what was familiar. I missed my family, but I also missed South Carolina. Although geographically, Florida is the South, culturally it is not. South Carolina is known for sweet tea, barbecue, shag music (our state's official dance is the Carolina Shag), tailgating at football games, nice people, going to church on Sundays, lovely ladies, gentlemen with manners, and family. People who grow up in the state rarely leave. And most who move away eventually come back. The culture and traditions draw you in, and once you experience them, you realize how blessed you are. This state—that I had been so anxious to get out of—was calling me back home and I couldn't wait any longer.

One of the worst parts of transferring from one school to another before your junior year is finding a roommate. Normally after two years of college you have a strong group of friends and two of you connect enough to want to room together. All of my friends were four hundred and fifty miles away. Thankfully I connected to a fellow ADPi named Kathryn who was transferring from the College of Charleston. The two of us talked on the phone for hours the summer before we started at USC. We became fast friends and that made the transition into a new school much easier. We decided we were going to live together and affiliate with ADPi at our new school.

I then moved to Nantucket with a high school friend for the summer. I got a job waitressing at two different restaurants, made a lot of money, and spent it all on rent. Nantucket is a beautiful island, but outrageously expensive for a college student. While I was there, Kathryn called informing me she didn't want to live on campus and had signed a lease to share an apartment with two other girls. That left me having to find a new roommate. A friend in ADPi at USC told me about another girl transferring into the sorority from the University of Florida. Her name was Clara and she was a sweet, southern girl from Beaufort, SC. I called her and we instantly hit it off and decided to room together. Once again God was working behind the scenes arranging things perfectly for His grand plan.

Clara had two guy friends she'd grown up with, Jeremy and Matt, who were always at our apartment. They were good people. We always had thought-provoking conversations and many of them were about God. They suggested the four of us do some kind of Bible study together. Before college I'd never done a Bible study of any kind. About the only Bible reading I'd ever done was a list of emergency verses printed on a purple bookmark that I kept in one of the Bibles my dad gave me. Emergency verses are those you read when something goes wrong, or you feel like it might. If you are in danger, you read Psalm 91. When you are depressed, read Psalms 34 and 139. When worried, read Philippians 4 . . . that sort of thing. It worked. When I was worried or down, in doubt or discouraged, I read the verses I was supposed to read. But that's about as far as my Bible knowledge went.

Clara, Jeremy, Matt, and I talked about what kind of Bible study to do, and none of us was quite sure because we didn't have a lot of experience with it. However, Chuck, another friend I met at USC, had a suggestion. Chuck was also a journalism major, but he was unlike anybody I'd ever met. The two of us spent a lot of time together studying and got to know each other very well. It was a strictly platonic relationship, as Chuck was in a very serious relationship with a precious girl who eventually became his wife. She was very well liked and had a strong Christian faith.

So did Chuck.

He had recently become close to God and his life changed dramatically. Apparently Chuck had a reputation on campus for being very social, to put it mildly. He had even won an award in his fraternity for being the biggest partier. But by the time I met him it seemed like all the stories were about someone else completely. I didn't have to dig very deep for him to tell me what had happened.

"God changed my life," Chuck told me.

I was intrigued. He was such a nice guy, talked favorably about his girlfriend, treated her with respect and love, and was one of the happiest people I had ever been around. I wanted what Chuck had, but I wasn't ready to give anything up to get it. Chuck went from literally dancing on the bar to reading his Bible and singing praise and worship music at the Fellowship of Christian Athletes meetings on campus. I wasn't ready to make such a radical life change. I wanted one foot in his world and one foot in mine. I still wanted to have fun, party, go to bars, and do everything most other college students did. Sure, I wanted God in my life, but some areas were off-limits to Him.

When I mentioned to Chuck that Matt, Jeremy, Clara, and I wanted to do a Bible study, he suggested a thirteen-week workbook by Henry Blackaby called *Experiencing God*. From the start I realized this wasn't going to be like any other book I'd worked through. I'd always believed that God wanted me to be a good person, and if I was good enough, He'd let me go to heaven when I died. The problem for me was, I never felt like I was good enough. When I looked at my life I knew I had disappointed God and let him down. I also felt helpless to change this. *Helpless* probably isn't the right word because that makes it sound like I tried to change and just couldn't. The problem was there were things I really liked doing, things of which I believed God did not approve. I still smoked. I still drank. And even though I wanted to get close to God I didn't want to give up anything to get there. All of this left me feeling like God remained very far away even as I tried getting closer to Him.

The first day of the first week of *Experiencing God* I learned a completely different way of thinking about God. I had grown up in church and I knew a lot about God, but I never understood how the Lord wanted to have an intimate, love relationship with me. Working with *Experiencing God*, I learned this relationship does not come through a program or a method or by keeping enough rules. The book challenged my idea of being a good person and attending church and hoping my efforts might be enough to win God's approval. Jesus did everything that needed to be done for me when He died on the cross and rose again three days later. Now, through His Son, God invited me to love Him just as He already loved me. I have to tell you, this rocked my world.

I'd be lying if I said that as soon as I read all of this I got down on my knees and asked God to take control of my life. However, He had my attention. I wanted to learn more. The next day I started working my way through the questions posed and the Scriptures quoted in the *Experiencing God* workbook. Day two compared people to pieces of clay in the hands of a potter. The potter works the clay and shapes it into what he wants it to be. In the same way God has molded and shaped each one of us and made us in a unique way so that we can serve Him. The book challenged me to open my eyes and see where God was already working in and around me. Knowing God and figuring out what He wanted to do in my life was as simple as surrendering control of my life to Him. He'd show me what he wanted me to do. His plan will be different for different people. Just like a potter forms some clay into a vase and some into a bowl, He makes all of us different to fulfill different purposes. All of this resonated with me. I was looking ahead to my future and trying to figure out what I should do with my life. This book gave me a way of finding the answers.

Clara, Jeremy, Matt, and I met once a week to talk about what we'd learned in the study. We were all pretty much at the same places in our lives and that made this group so meaningful to me. No one acted like they had all this God stuff figured out. The ideas in this book were new to most of us. And God was moving in the life of each one of us. Even today I consider this the best Bible study I've ever done.

In the middle of my journey into *Experiencing God* a friend invited me to go as his date to the Sigma Alpha Epsilon fraternity's Mountain Weekend. I don't know if mountain weekends are a part of Greek culture all over the country or only in the Southeast, but at South Carolina it was a big deal to be invited. It was like being asked to prom. SAE was one of my favorite fraternities on campus because so many of my male friends were members. My grandfather and cousin were SAEs at USC and all the boys reminded me of them or my own dad. They were nice, handsome, and a lot of fun. They all grew up in families like mine and I knew many of them because our parents were friends. So when an SAE boy invites you to be his date, you say yes without hesitation. The weekend is always a blast. The fraternity rented a bus and everyone piled in it together. We drove a few hours up to the mountains and drank beer, played music, and partied all the way to our destination. The aisle of the bus was always filled with decorated coolers that were gifts from the girls. I spent hours painting coolers and cups for my dates over the years and always wanted to present the best, most decorative cooler. The girls painted the coolers with their fraternity letters, their mascot (the SAEs were the lions), and used their fraternity colors. My sorority, ADPi, was also a lion and our colors were azure blue and white. We were the first official sorority in the country. Guys on campus told me, "The ADPis are smart and the marrying type." I was very protective of my reputation when it came to boys. I was a lot of fun, but was not promiscuous. Plus, I was a new student at USC and wanted guys to know I was not THAT kind of girl. However, I knew that at Mountain Weekend, I was going to be sharing a bedroom with my date. I didn't feel comfortable about this. My date was only a friend, not someone I planned to get involved with romantically.

I wasn't sure what to do, so I called my friend Eden, my Christian friend at Wake Forest University whom I'd met making my debut. She had gone on Mountain Weekends and understood the importance of being asked and accepting the invitation. She was very supportive and gave me some good, Christian advice—to basically be a lady and don't do anything you would regret later. She was always the perfect balance of good and fun. Everyone knew how important her faith was, but she was still in the popular crowd and every friend looked up to her.

I also wanted a guy's advice. I went to Chuck and asked him, "What should I do?" He'd gone on mountain weekends before his life changed.

"I don't think you should go," he answered.

"Chuck! That is not an option," I said. "I'm going." I wasn't asking him whether or not I should go. I wanted him to help me figure out a way to navigate the weekend in a righteous way, since I would be spending an entire weekend in a coed cabin.

Since Chuck didn't have any helpful advice, I did what Eden suggested. When my date and I arrived at the mountain weekend I told him, "Listen, I really appreciate you asking me to come on this trip and I hope I'm not going to be a disappointment to you but God's really working on my heart and I'm doing a Bible study right now. In fact, I brought it with me."

"Yeah, yeah, that's cool," he said. "My mom's a really strong Christian."

"If you want to, I'm going to go outside and do one of the

lessons. You can do it with me if you want," I said. He didn't act like I was crazy, which was such a relief. The next morning I got up and did my Bible study outside. My friend, and even my date, joined me.

That night the entire party moved into the cabin where my date and I were staying because it was the senior cabin. Music blared. A fire was going. I could smell marijuana. Everyone was drinking and laughing at things that suddenly struck me as inappropriate. I sat there, a drink in my hand, watching everything going on around me as if I were having an out-of-body experience. The walls nearly shook because the music and voices were so loud. But, for me, it was like the sound just shut off and a hush filled the room. Instead of being in the middle of the fun I found myself thinking, *What would Jesus think if He walked in right now? And what would MY DAD think!?* I thought about all the Christians in my life whom I adored and wondered what they would do in this situation.

I got up and walked out onto the back steps. I stared out at the snow falling in the woods while the party blared behind me. I wanted to pray, but suddenly I wasn't sure how. Someone had once told me that when you don't know how to pray, just say what is on your mind, like talking to a friend. That's what I did.

*God, I don't know how to do this but I want you in my life. I am willing to give up all of this, the smoking and the drinking and everything else. You must already be taking that away from me because I don't want to do it anymore. I want whatever else is out there. I want this void in my life filled forever . . . I want it filled with you.*

The only way I can describe what happened next is to say that I had been trapped at the bottom of a slimy pit and no matter how hard I tried to grip the sides and climb out, I kept falling in deeper. But on October 19, 1997, sitting on the back steps of the mountain weekend house with snow falling around me, I felt God throw down a rope ladder and help me out of that pit once and for all. This was what I had been searching for all of my life.

THE WEEKEND ENDED. On the drive down the mountain toward home I knew my life was never going to be the same. I felt lighter. Clean. Free. I kept thanking God over and over for getting me through the weekend and changing my life. When I got home the first Bible verse I read was 2 Corinthians 5:17, which says, "Therefore, if anyone is in Christ, the new creation has come: The old has gone, the new is here!" That was me. I was a new woman. I memorized that verse. It was the first verse I'd ever tried to memorize.

The next Sunday I went to church with some of the girls from my sorority. I discovered that about half of the girls in ADPi were strong Christians. One of them, Michelle, invited me to join her at a Baptist church where the college ministry was so large it had to meet in the movie theater next door. We sat up front. Michelle asked me to sit next to her. Before the praise band came out she leaned over and said, "I heard you did a Bible study at SAE's mountain weekend." Apparently, word had gotten out about me.

"I did," I told her. Then I told her about surrendering everything to God and the new relationship I had with Him.

"That's amazing," Michelle said. "I know a lot of people are going to give you grief over this, but don't worry about them. Your life has changed already but it is now going to change in ways you don't expect. A lot of your friendships are going to change. People are going to pull away from you."

"Really?" I said. All my life I'd tried to be a friend to everyone.

When I was in high school and running for a student-council position, I was handing out campaign literature about myself and one girl told me she didn't like me because she thought I was a prep. I was crushed that someone could judge me for no reason. Now Michelle was telling me that I could expect a lot more rejection because of the change in my life. Couldn't people see my heart and know that I was always pursuing kindness and trying to love others?

"They aren't going to like what you are doing. They won't think you are fun anymore, but they will always look up to you and respect you," Michelle continued. Then she added, "Those are also the ones who are going to come to you when they are going through their darkest days."

Michelle was right on both counts. All my friends with whom I used to party didn't want to hang out with a Bible beater. That was all right with me because this Bible beater wanted to hang out with other people who loved Jesus. I just wanted to submerge myself completely in God and learn as much as I could about Him and get as close to Him as I could. I still loved my former friends, but my life had changed. (Most of them are now moms and see the importance in knowing Christ, but they found Him after college, as many do.) Every time I went to church I cried through the worship time. These were tears of joy for the change that God had made in my life but also tears of grief for all the time I'd wasted.

I also started attending the Fellowship of Christian Athletes. I wasn't an athlete but that was okay with everyone at FCA. You don't have to play a sport to go. For me, I just wanted to be wherever people were talking about Jesus and studying the Bible and worshiping Him. I started buying Christian music CDs. Up until that point the only Christian singer I'd heard of was Amy Grant. I found there were hundreds of Christian singers and groups! One time I mentioned a new song to a guy I started dating and he laughed at me. "That song's been around forever," he said, laughing.

"Well, I have never heard it before," I said.

Of all the people I told about my new relationship with Jesus, the hardest turned out to be my family. I thought they would be thrilled because here's their daughter who's no longer partying and smoking but instead is studying and dating good, Christian men. Their initial reaction surprised me. Now that I'm a mother myself, though, I get it, but I didn't at the time. From their point of view a daughter had stopped going to the formal church where she'd grown up and instead was going to a more extreme church and was talking openly about something that had always been a private matter in our family. Basically, my mother's reaction to my saying I was now a Christian was, "What do you mean *now*? We raised you as a Christian in a Christian home attending a Christian church. We believe Jesus is the Son of God. How can you say that you weren't a Christian before?" These weren't her exact words but it was the essence of what she said in the many discussions the two of us had about this.

All I could do in response was to assure her that I knew all of this was true and that I was thankful for how I'd been brought up, but that something was still missing. And that something was a *personal* relationship with Jesus, of knowing Him and experiencing Him.

Some of you reading this may have the same reaction as my parents. Or you may think this chapter is very preachy for a news anchor to be writing. I do not mean to preach. I'm simply telling you honestly what happened to me. When I came to Jesus I found someone who loves me, not someone who condemns me. That's what I hope to convey to you as well. I didn't write this chapter to make anyone feel guilty or inadequate. Instead I just wanted to share with you why I am who I am. At a weekend that was supposed to be one of the biggest frat parties ever, my life changed because of Jesus. I love Him so much for what He has done for me. He loves you too. If you don't take anything else away from this chapter, I hope you will hear that. God loves you.

# 4

## Getting a Grip on Grace

> As a father has compassion on his children, so the Lord
> has compassion on those who fear him; for he knows
> how we are formed, he remembers that we are dust.
>
> —PSALM 103:13–14

NOT LONG AGO my daughter insisted on holding my water
bottle. I tried to reason with her and explain how it was
too heavy for her but you can't reason with a one-year-old. Then I
tried to bargain with her by offering to pour some water into her
sippy cup. Hayden wasn't having any of it. She shook her head
back and forth and said, "Hold it? Hold it?"

Finally I gave in. "Okay, you can hold it. What do you say?"
Hayden rubbed her hand on her chest, which is sign language for
*please* and said, "Please." I placed the bottle in her hands but tried
to hold them in mine to keep her from dropping it.

"NO! Hayden hold it," she said as she jerked the bottle away
from me. Just as I had warned her, when she tried to take a drink
she poured freezing-cold water down her chest, soaking her little
body as she sat strapped in her high chair. As I hurriedly tried to
get her unbuckled, she screamed in pain.

I lifted Hayden out of her high chair. "You're okay, you're okay,"
I said, trying to soothe her, but she screamed and cried even louder. I
pulled her dress off and wrapped her in a towel. Cradling her to my
chest, I rubbed her, warming her up. "I know it's very cold. That's
why Momma didn't want you to hold it. I was trying to protect you,
my love." Hayden placed her head against me, still sobbing.

As I sat in my kitchen, holding my shivering daughter, I saw myself in her. I have a heavenly Father who loves me, but for most of my first twenty-one years, I did not listen to Him and did things my way. Inevitably, I'd end up shivering and cold, crying out to Him as I suffered the consequences of my poor choices. But I kept dumping freezing-cold water on myself because all I could think about was everything I might have to renounce if I gave Him complete control of my life. Even though He tries to protect us, and we know His ways are higher than ours, we still try to do things our way, thinking we know best. Now, with a daughter of my own who doesn't like the rules I have set for her, I see God in a new light. I realize He really does have my own best interests at heart because He loves me so much. That's a lesson it's taken me a long time to learn.

God had my best interests at heart when He nudged me to change majors and colleges. Before, I struggled not only to keep up with all my science classes, I also struggled to stay interested. My biology classes went well but I hated chemistry and it hated me. We were not a good match. That just fed the growing sense of discontent within me, that feeling like something needed to change. Deep down, I knew that dental school was also a poor match for me, but my practical planner side kept me locked into that decision. And I *am* a planner. My life is scheduled and regimented. I don't like leaving anything to chance. I think that's what caused me to go ahead with the biology major/orthodontist plan. My future was laid out and I was assured of having a good career and a comfortable life.

As I have always heard, people plan and God laughs. I think during my two years at FSU God must have been looking down at me, shaking His head and laughing: *Ainsley, this just isn't you*. But when I started my journalism course, I felt the exact opposite. I'd found my place even though I was busier than I'd ever been in my life. Anytime you change majors you lose hours, which can push back graduation. If you transfer from one college to another, you lose even more hours and graduation gets pushed back even further. I did both. My dad told my siblings and me, he would cover four years of college and no more. After this, I'd be lucky if I graduated in five. I had no choice but to jump in with both feet and take as many credit hours as I could. Once you paid for twelve hours, the rest were free, so I loaded up. I was trying to make up for lost time. Being so busy, though, did have a bright side: I didn't have time to eat much more than a bagel with a glass of sweet tea for lunch, which meant my dad didn't have to pay for a full meal plan. At least I saved him a little money.

I approached school like a girl on a mission and used my organizational skills to get through my studies. Keeping everything straight wasn't easy but I figured out a system to organize all of my notes. I also did my homework assignments every night. Most professors checked and gave you a 100/A+ test grade at the end of the semester if you did all of the homework. That was a no-brainer for me. In fact, I thought it determined who would and would not be successful in life. There were many talented kids who never did their homework. I thought that was a sign of laziness. Why wouldn't you take advantage of an easy A? The homework also prepared me for the big exams, especially in math. Midterms and finals were always mastered by studying and reviewing every single homework assignment. When I had to study for my exams, I went back over my homework and redid every math problem. Similar math problems were, of course, on the exam, and if I knew how to do one, I knew how to do them all. The key was studying in advance. That was the key then and still is today.

Now, every day I anchor a three-hour morning show, and I have to be prepared. Most of the hours is ad-libbing and talking off the cuff about the main news stories of the day. I prepare like I'm getting ready for a test in college. I spend at least an hour alone in my office before each show getting organized. I write every big news topic on the outside of a manila folder and put bullet points under each topic. That way it's all in front of me, in one place, and easy for me to see if I need to glance down during the show. This is essentially the same system I used in college. It worked then and it still works today.

From the time I arrived at the University of South Carolina I was determined to go far and didn't want anything to stand in my way. I juggled my classes and my social life and tried to be a better person. After October 19, 1997, my relationship with God became my highest priority. In Psalm 63:1 the psalmist says that he thirsts for God and that his whole being longs for Him. That's how I felt. At FCA meetings there were good friends, great worship, and phenomenal speakers. I got so excited about FCA that when I was nominated for homecoming queen and had to make a speech onstage, all I did was talk about FCA. I was supposed to answer a question posed to me by the judges, but I was nervous and pretty much ignored it. Instead I said, "God is my Savior and He's changed me and I'm very involved in Fellowship of Christian Athletes and if you haven't experienced it you really need to come to one of our meetings because you will learn so much about Christ and His love." That answer had nothing to do with the question, which was really embarrassing. I should have listened more closely to the judges, but I was happy to glorify God. I didn't win the homecoming crown. I was named first or second runner-up. I honestly can't remember exactly. I just knew I wasn't the queen, but I was happy to serve God, my king.

After I finished the *Experiencing God* study I dove into other Bible studies. I also bought a new Bible (the New International Version) and began reading it constantly and made notes in it like

I never had before. Church suddenly became much more interesting and the pastor's sermons hit home. Many times I felt like he was talking only to me. I took notes through every sermon because I wanted to grow closer to Christ and soak up everything I felt I had missed. As I have said, I cried through every church service for the first year after I was saved. I just felt so much grief over the twenty-one years I'd wasted. At the same time I felt a huge sense of relief and gratitude that I was still only twenty-one and had my entire life to live for Him. I also felt an obligation to dive deeper. I prayed specifically for everyone I met who needed healing, love, good health, financial freedom, less stress—you name it and I prayed for it. Everyone who came to me I felt was a gift from God, and I was supposed to hear their story and add them to my prayer list. I spent hours in "the Word" (scripture) every day and wrote in my journal constantly. I still have a huge box with all of them. I wrote personalized notes to friends who were hurting and spent all the money I could spare in the Christian bookstore buying gifts to help others. I bought countless Bibles for people who were interested in learning more and invited so many people to church, FCA, and other Christian activities. It was contagious and I wanted others to experience the same love. I had a heart for other people who were in pain and wanted them to find the same freedom I found in Christ.

God's timing could not have been better. It's no coincidence that I finally surrendered my life and future plans to Him in the middle of a Bible study called *Experiencing God: Knowing and Doing the Will of God.* When I started it I wanted to get closer to God, but I was also trying to figure out exactly what I should do with the rest of my life. God met me in both places. He'd been knocking on the door of my heart for a while. Back in high school those anonymous letters ("from God") had continued to show up in my mailbox. Another one read:

*Dear Friend,*
*How are you? I just had to send a note to tell you how*
*much I care about you. I saw you yesterday as you were*
*talking with your friends. I waited all day hoping you*
*would want to talk to me too. I gave you a sunset to chase*
*your day and a cool breeze to rest you—and I waited. You*
*never came. It hurt me—but I still love you because I am*
*your friend.*

*I saw you sleeping last night and long to touch your*
*brow, so I spilled moonlight upon your face. Again I*
*waited, wanting to rush down so we could talk.*

*I have so many gifts for you! I try to tell you in the blue*
*skies and in the quiet green grass. I whisper it in leaves on*
*the trees and breathe it in colors of flowers, shout it to you*
*in mountain streams, give the birds love songs to sing. I*
*clothe you with warm sunshine and perfume the air with*
*nature scents. My love for you is deeper than the ocean and*
*bigger than the biggest need in your heart.*

*Ask me! Talk with me! Please don't forget me. I have so*
*much to share with you! I have chosen you and I will wait*
*for you.*

*Your friend,*
*Jesus*

Talk about an invitation from God Himself to get closer to
Him! When I opened the letter and read it, I felt so sad. I had
neglected God. He knew it and I knew it. I had no idea who God
nudged or told to send this letter to me. Just like all the others,
there was no return address, and therefore I couldn't respond, but
it clearly impacted my life and I saved it forever. Little did I know
there were more to come.

Months later this one arrived:

*When Christ was on the cross you were on His mind.*

Another one followed:

*Lord, remind me that nothing is going to happen today that you and I can't handle together.*

It wasn't until I sat down to write this book that I realized the person who sent these letters to me was most likely my dad. I have never asked him, but he was always encouraging me to get closer to Christ, read my Bible, and say my prayers. He saw the need and so did I. I just felt like I didn't have the right tools. I was too busy having fun and doing my own thing. Yet, when I was ready, God met me there. His timing was perfect.

The summer after my junior year of college I interned at WIS-TV in Columbia and lived at home. After my fourth year I interned at WCBD, Channel 2 in Charleston, and lived with my sister. She lived in an old, historic, three-bedroom home downtown on Smith Street. She agreed to let me share a room with her because the other rooms were occupied by roommates. The two of us slept in her full-size bed in a room that had space only for the bed and a chest of drawers. Needless to say, we had a few arguments (as all sisters do) and before the summer was over she tried to kick me out three times.

The house itself was sometimes a source of the drama. No matter how nice a house in Charleston may be, large roaches find a way to surprise you regularly. One morning I pulled back the shower curtain when I was getting ready for work and saw the largest palmetto bug (SC is the Palmetto State) staring me in the face. I screamed and am sure I ran in the opposite direction. I hate roaches and am terrified of alligators.

Crime was also an issue in downtown Charleston. One day

while getting dressed in the bathroom I looked out the window and saw a man up in the tree watching me. I was so shaken that I called the police. The man was long gone when they arrived. Another morning I walked outside to get in my car and the window was shattered. Glass covered the sidewalk and my passenger-side seat. The brick someone used to smash my window was also sitting on the seat. My radio/CD player was gone.

Even with the bugs in the shower, the creep in the tree, and the car break-in, my summer interning at WCBD was one of the best summers of my life. I learned so much working at the TV station, which gave me confidence to move forward as a journalist. At that time one of the station's top anchors and reporters was Amy Robach. She graciously allowed me to tag along with her each day in the field and watch her interview people; she even allowed me to shoot stand-ups for my résumé tape. I stood in front of the camera and ad-libbed a script, pretending to be on TV while the cameraman recorded it. Amy now works on *Good Morning America* not far from where I work at Fox News. The two of us are both on television at the same time every morning. That makes me smile. We both made it to the number one market and I am indebted to her forever. She taught me the fundamentals of broadcasting, took me under her wing, and made time for me when she didn't have to. Amy had a big impact on my life.

I WAS SO young, only twenty-two, when I started that internship in Charleston. My dad's parents lived in Columbia too and I enjoyed being able to visit them regularly. My mom's parents had both recently passed away, and losing them, especially my first grandparent, Mimi, my mom's mom, was excruciating. I was still in college and had just transferred to South Carolina when Mimi and Pop broke the news to us that Mimi had been diagnosed with colon cancer. I had never experienced loss and she was the healthiest and youngest of all four of my grandparents. This was not supposed to happen to her.

Even though Mimi and Pop lived two hours away in Greenville, they were extremely involved in our lives. They spoiled us and made each of their six grandchildren feel like he or she was their favorite. Pop was tough, but loving. He was the disciplinarian. Pop served our country in the Navy during World War II. Once I interviewed him for a class project and he told me the story about a Kamikaze pilot who was on a suicide mission and headed straight for his ship. The pilot looked at the seamen on the top deck (my grandfather was one of them), gave them a peace sign with his fingers and crashed his plane into the ocean instead of my grandfather's ship. Thank goodness. My grandfather's life was spared.

When Pop came home from the war he and his best friend went to work at the local Coca-Cola bottling company. The two of them started at the bottom, bottling Cokes. My grandfather worked his way all the way up to an executive vice presidency, while his best friend became president.

Once you walked into Mimi and Pop's home, you knew he was affiliated with Coke. They had a Tiffany chandelier with Coca-Cola written around its circumference and a red metal Coca-Cola cooler filled with every sort of Coca-Cola product from Cokes and Fanta to Fresca. When you turned the corner and went upstairs into the kitchen, the red breadbox had Coca-Cola written across it in white and the radio in the bathroom was a mini Coca-Cola drink machine. No one in the family was allowed to drink Pepsi, not that we wanted to. Pop said Coke only, and what Pop said was gospel. We followed his rules.

If he saw someone wearing a baseball cap during the national anthem at a South Carolina football game, he reached over and flicked it right off their head. He was very respectful and expected others to be the same. He was old enough and wise enough to earn the respect of everyone who met him.

Pop loved my grandmother and she took pride in caring for her household. She always looked her best and her home was her joy. I guess by today's standards their home was small, but my grandparents were so thankful for it, and when I was a little girl it seemed huge. The split level made it seem like a three-story house. Everything in the house matched and the whole place was perfectly organized, even the closets. My grandmother wrapped all her shoes in tissue paper and lined them up in the closet in their original boxes. I used to stand and watch Mimi do her makeup each morning as she stood at her dresser, using the mirror above the furniture. Her top drawer was full of containers of makeup. I always got into her lipsticks, which were labeled and perfectly placed. The back bedroom was my mom's. It was painted in a very pale blue color, which, of course, matched the comforter and pillows. The bookshelves were full of the classics and Mimi's Bible-study workbooks from years prior. Inside the books she'd made copious notes and highlighted passages. It wasn't until she passed away that I realized how much she loved the Lord. She was very private about her faith. Those books eventually made it onto the bookshelves in my childhood bedroom at my parents' house.

I loved going to Mimi and Pop's house because it was a happy place. They never spoke an ill word about anyone, at least not around me. Mimi's motto (and eventually my mom's motto) was, "If you can't say anything nice, don't say it at all." My grandmother was one of the few people I felt understood me.

And now she was dying.

I didn't understand it. She ate better than anyone I knew and was the picture of health. We never expected her to get sick.

Every day she weighed herself. If she ever went over her usual 103 pounds she cut back on her eating until her weight dropped back to normal. All in all she'd never had any kind of real health problems until she started feeling bad one day. Then came the doctor's diagnosis. And then the phone call.

The illness progressed quickly. I tried to spend as much time with her as I could, but with my school schedule that became more and more difficult. However, I made the time. On one of her last days I drove up to Greenville just to sit with her in the hospital and talk. And that's all we did. We talked like she wasn't sick and she was going to live forever. They say when someone you love is dying you should let them know that it's okay for them to go. I wanted to do that, but at the same time, selfishly, I couldn't bear the thought of not having her in my life. I didn't want to let her go. Her Presbyterian minister came into the room and prayed at her bedside. I listened as they talked. At one point he started reciting Scripture. My grandmother recited it verbatim with him. I never knew she'd memorized Scripture. She never let on. She never told me. I should have known. My grandmother didn't talk a lot about her faith, but she lived it every day.

A day or so later I had to say my good-byes. I remember feeling a sense of peace knowing she would be with Jesus soon and I would see her again. My mother and aunt spent every waking hour in the hospital room with her. They took turns sleeping in the chair or the cot the nurses had brought in for them. They played cards and sat by their mother until she took her last breath. To say it was a sad moment is a huge understatement. To this day no one in our family can talk about it without tearing up. I'm writing this twenty years later and I still have tears streaming down my face. At Mimi's funeral the minister read this passage from the book of Proverbs:

A wife of noble character who can find?
　　She is worth far more than rubies.
Her husband has full confidence in her
　　and lacks nothing of value.
She brings him good, not harm,
　　all the days of her life.
She selects wool and flax
　　and works with eager hands.
She is like the merchant ships,
　　bringing her food from afar.
She gets up while it is still night;
　　she provides food for her family
and portions for her female servants.
　　She considers a field and buys it;
out of her earnings she plants a vineyard.
　　She sets about her work vigorously;
her arms are strong for her tasks.
　　She sees that her trading is profitable,
and her lamp does not go out at night.
　　In her hand she holds the distaff
and grasps the spindle with her fingers.
　　She opens her arms to the poor
and extends her hands to the needy.
　　When it snows, she has no fear for her household;
for all of them are clothed in scarlet.
　　She makes coverings for her bed;
she is clothed in fine linen and purple.
　　Her husband is respected at the city gate,
where he takes his seat among the elders of the land.
　　She makes linen garments and sells them,
and supplies the merchants with sashes.
　　She is clothed with strength and dignity;

she can laugh at the days to come.

She speaks with wisdom,
and faithful instruction is on her tongue.

She watches over the affairs of her household
and does not eat the bread of idleness.

Her children arise and call her blessed;
her husband also, and he praises her:

"Many women do noble things,
but you surpass them all."

Charm is deceptive, and beauty is fleeting;
but a woman who fears the Lord is to be praised.

Honor her for all that her hands have done,
and let her works bring her praise at the city gate.

—PROVERBS 31:10–31

This passage perfectly described my Mimi. She was the picture of a "Proverbs 31 woman." Listening to the minister read these words made me miss her even more, and thank God for her at the same time. But the words did more than that. I decided at that point to make her proud, be the best I could be, and do well in the broadcasting field. I knew I wanted to work in a top-ten news market someday or at the national level. Reflecting on my grandmother's life, I also had another goal. I wanted my character to be like hers. I, too, wanted to be a Proverbs 31 woman. Charm *is* deceptive. And beauty *is* fleeting. But a woman who fears, serves, and loves the Lord will be praised. No matter what else I may accomplish in my life, that is the praise I long for above all else.

# 5

## *"Reporting Live for WLTX . . ."*

Whatever you do, do it all for the glory of God.

—1 CORINTHIANS 10:31

DURING MY FINAL semester at South Carolina I got my first taste of what it was going to be like to actually work in broadcast journalism. The university had both a radio and television station, all manned by students. I rotated between the two, working every position possible. That meant I worked as director one day and the camera operator the next. Or I chased a story as a reporter and came back to anchor the newscast at 4 P.M. When I reported on a story for the campus television station I took the camera out, lined up my interviews, and then figured out the best angle to set the camera up on a tripod, pushed the record button, and jumped in front of the camera for my stand-up. We called that a one-man band. Back at the studio I had to write the script, cut the sound bites of the people I interviewed, edit the piece, and then get myself ready to go on the air. Other days I hosted the radio show or worked in the control room on the soundboard. Basically, during that final semester I did anything and everything I might one day need to do to land a job. It was the hardest semester I'd had, but it was also the best preparation for what was to come. I called it my first real job.

Since I was on track to graduate in December, I thought that gave me a leg up on those who graduated in May in terms of finding a job. I really wanted to work in a big market in the Northeast, a place like New York, but I knew I would have to start off at a smaller station and make my mistakes before heading to Manhattan. I planned to put together a résumé tape with multiple on-camera reports, make copies, then send it out to news directors at television stations across the country around the first of the year. One of my professors, though, had other ideas.

Right before the Thanksgiving break, Dr. Sonya Duhé asked me where I was planning on applying for on-air positions. I explained that I was going to search outside of South Carolina. She shook her head. "You need to go visit news directors at local stations, and you need to do it during the Thanksgiving break."

Now I was the one shaking my head. "Dr. Duhé, I don't want to stay in South Carolina. I've lived here my entire life. I want to go somewhere else." Deep down I still had dreams of living in New York or California.

"You don't have a choice," she replied. "I'm your professor and I'm telling you to do this!"

I did as I was told. I sent résumé tapes to news directors in Savannah, Charleston, and Columbia. Although Savannah is in Georgia, not South Carolina, it is just across the border and the station had an excellent reputation. After sending out the tapes I called all the stations and asked if I could stop by and get some advice. I didn't want to ask, "Will you hire me?" over the phone. I thought I had a better shot if they saw my drive and enthusiasm face-to-face. Most of the news directors invited me to come in for a talk. My boyfriend and I borrowed my mom's car and visited each station.

My professor was right. Going around to all the local stations worked. I received a job offer from the Charleston station where I'd completed an internship the summer before. Another Charleston station offered me a job with the stipulation that it was technically part-time. The station manager explained that I would work nearly forty hours a week, but he needed me to be a part-time employee so he didn't have to pay my health insurance. The Savannah station was also interested in me. The news director told me he was trying to put together an offer for me but he wasn't sure when he could actually do it. He even called Dr. Duhé and told her that he definitely planned on hiring me.

The response from the news director at the Columbia station, Larry Audas, wasn't nearly as encouraging. When I called to try to set up an appointment with him, all he said was, "Go get two years of experience and then call me." It looked like I was going to have to choose between Charleston or Savannah, both beautiful cities, both wonderful places to live, but both small markets in terms of television news.

A week after the Thanksgiving break, Dr. Duhé called Larry Audas and invited him to come to the university to critique our four o'clock live news broadcast. There were probably fifteen to twenty of us in the class and we each had different responsibilities during the newscast. As soon as it was over, Larry pulled me and another girl aside and said he wanted to interview us for his station. I nearly laughed. The man who told me to go get two years of experience was now asking me to come in for an interview. WLTX News-19 was a middle-size market. If I got the offer, I knew it would be a great opportunity and something I probably couldn't turn down.

I was a nervous wreck leading up to my interview. I sought all the advice and encouragement I could get. My then boyfriend drove me to the appointment. As I got out of the car he looked at me and said, "I hope you know, they need you as much as you need them." That boost of confidence really helped me. I never forgot that advice. I never thought I was perfect, but I needed to be reminded that I too had something to offer: my work ethic, my positive attitude, and my drive.

Larry Audas, bless his heart, offered me the job that day. He gave me a shot. That meant I had three offers and I needed to make a decision. My professors said there were four factors that I needed to pay attention to: the company, the position, the market size, and the pay. The company is important because not all media companies are created equal and some large corporations like Gannett and Cox own stations across the country. That makes jobs at such stations appealing because you can move to a larger market while remaining with the same company and keep the same benefits and 401(k). The market size is determined by the number of people who can turn on their TVs and watch that station. New York is the largest and, at last check, Glendive, Montana, was the smallest. The larger the market, the more visibility you receive, which can open doors to move to even larger markets or to a national news program.

The pay, the last factor, was similar between the two full-time offers, although each had different benefits. When I weighed each job offer, the best fit seemed to be in Columbia, my hometown. The company, Gannett, was large, well-known, and owned stations all over the country; the market size was better than the other two offers (Columbia is number seventy-nine in market size, Charleston's is ninety-nine, and Savannah is ninety-six at last check); and the schedule was unbelievable for a young, college graduate. Larry asked me to report for the late-night newscast at eleven, Sundays through Thursdays, which meant I had Fridays and Saturdays off. The pay was also a little better than the others. I made $24,000 my first year with the promise of a thousand-dollar pay raise each year. At the time I was working as a waitress at Za's Pizza, making a lot less. I was excited to finally get a salary.

A few days after my last interview I called Larry Audas to accept his offer. He brought my contract over for me to sign that night while I was working at the pizza place. I still have the photograph of me dressed in my waitress outfit, signing my very first contract at the bar at Za's Pizza. I have taken a picture of me signing every contract since. That day, at Za's, I was overjoyed. I was now officially a reporter for WLTX in my hometown, this was my first real job, and I finally had a salary. I could not wait to get started.

I WAS UNDERSTANDABLY nervous on my first day on the job. When I arrived Larry showed me around the office and introduced me to all my new coworkers. Everyone was polite and made me feel welcome. After this, Larry showed me my cubicle, where I would work and write my scripts. Then he escorted me into the storage closet, which was filled with pens, stacks of paper, memo pads, sticky notes, highlighters, calendars, and every other office supply imaginable.

"Take whatever you want," he said.

Now, office supplies might seem ordinary to most people, but my eyes lit up. I was in heaven. When I was a little girl I loved shopping for school supplies or crafts. I had an art table in my room for all of my creative projects. In seventh grade I spent hours at that table making earrings out of watercolor paper, paints, and hot glue and sold them at school, at Dr. Boyd's office, and at various boutiques at the beach. My company was called Ainsley's Art, which was written out in gold paint on the top of each card that held two earrings. I displayed them in a thick, heavy, white Christmas-present box I found in my parents' attic, and sold the most at school. My teachers loved them. This was the late eighties and watercolor, paper earrings were very popular. The moment I walked into the WLTX storage closet and was told to take whatever I wanted, I felt like that twelve-year-old girl in a craft store all over again.

The first story I ever covered was a ride-along with the local sheriff's department. The officers gave me and the cameraman bulletproof vests, which was both frightening and exciting. We rode through the streets of a neighborhood known for crime near Williams-Brice Stadium. We immediately saw something suspicious. The cameras were rolling as the deputies chased after a man who was allegedly caught in a drug bust. The officers finally caught up with the suspect and tackled him to the ground. I had to watch the whole thing from the car because the officers said it was too dangerous, but my heart was pounding. I saw it all. They didn't bring the suspect straight back to the car, however. When the deputies came back I asked one, "What's going on?"

"We're gonna have to take this suspect to the hospital," he said.

"Why?" I asked. "Is he hurt?"

"No. We're going to have to do a body-cavity search," he replied.

"A what?" I asked.

"He hid the drugs up his rear end," the deputy said. "Happens all the time."

When I did the news report that night I did not mention where the drugs ended up. That's too much information for most viewers. But I did call my mom and told her, "Mom, I went on this drug bust and you will never guess what this guy did with the drugs!" My first day was over and it was thrilling. I enjoyed knowing everything that really went on, not just what the public hears. I knew I'd picked the right profession.

Not every day was as enlightening. One day a report came across the police radio that the Summit neighborhood was on lockdown because an old hand grenade had been discovered in the ground. Everyone in the neighborhood was on edge, wondering if more were going to be found. Police warned residents not to pull the pins if they found any. My boss told me to go into the neighborhood and cover the story. Before I left the station I contacted the police and got as much information as possible. Then we headed out. Ideally, in situations like this, I might find someone in the neighborhood willing to talk on-camera.

When we pulled into the area no one was outside. If I was going to get an interview I would have to find someone the only way I knew how. I started knocking on people's doors hoping to get a resident's perspective. I walked up on a porch and saw a chow dog tied to a rocking chair. That made me think the owners were home. When I got near the glass storm door I saw a woman inside. As soon as I knocked the chow lunged toward me. I jumped back and reminded myself that he was tied to the chair. But that didn't stop the dog. He took off after me, dragging the rocking chair behind him. I leaped off the porch and ran out into the yard, the dog and rocking chair right behind me. The dog managed to take a bite out of me before I jumped back into the car.

Back at the station, I cleaned and bandaged the wound and returned to the story. I was supposed to interview a man named Tom who worked for the South Carolina Department of Health and Environmental Control. Tom immediately noticed I was a little out of sorts. "How are you doing?" he asked. "Is everything okay?"

"I'm a little shaken up because I was just bitten by a dog," I said.

"What?" he replied.

"A dog bit me when I tried to get some interviews for the grenade story. I still can't believe it."

"Where is the dog?" he asked.

"I'm guessing back on the front porch with its rocking chair out in the Summit neighborhood," I said.

Tom said, "Ainsley, I'm afraid you told the wrong person. I'm going to have to have that dog put in quarantine. State law. Anytime a dog bites somebody it is put into quarantine for a period of time to make sure it doesn't have rabies."

I'm sure the lady who wouldn't answer her door hated me after that. The dog didn't have rabies, thank goodness. From then on, I always checked porches for dogs before knocking on doors.

That dog wasn't the only dangerous animal I came across in my early news stories. One day my news director told me to go check out a report that a woman's pet tiger had gotten out of its cage and was spotted walking down the street. The tiger's owner agreed to do an on-camera interview to tell her side of the story. I didn't hesitate. My cameraman and I went straight to the woman's house. She seemed eager to talk. After telling us how her tiger was a great cat, which she had raised from a cub, and how he wouldn't hurt anyone, she asked, "Would you like to meet him?"

"Sure," I said.

The next thing I knew I was inside a cage with a full-grown tiger! Never in a million years would I do that today, but at the time I didn't hesitate. My boss told me to get the story and I was determined to make it unforgettable. The woman entered the cage and I followed. She kept talking about how the tiger was just an oversized house cat. Even when he came over close to me she said something like, "Oh, he just wants to play." I bent down to get a better look at this exquisite, strong animal and the tiger playfully locked my arm in his jaws. It was a light bite and barely broke the skin, but he definitely got my attention. I was young, invincible, and willing to go the distance to get a story, but I was also ready to tell the woman's overgrown house cat good-bye.

WHEN I STARTED at WLTX I reported for the eleven o'clock news, which meant I didn't have to go in to work until three in the afternoon. It was a great schedule for many reasons. The night owl that I am loved staying up late and having my mornings to sleep in or just take care of personal business. Most nights I got off work between midnight and one. I had moved back in with my parents to save money and instead of going straight home, I usually stopped by my boyfriend's apartment to talk or wind down after a long day. His apartment was very close to my parents' home. He moved there to be closer to me even though it was about fifteen minutes away from the downtown university area.

For most college graduates, moving back in with mom and dad is great financially, but it's hard to live under their rules again. This was the case for me. For one thing, our schedules didn't mesh very well. My dad still came into my room in the morning, threw open the shutters, and announced, "If I'm up, you're up," like he did when I was a little girl. For a twenty-two-year-old college graduate who didn't get home from work until the middle of the night, being awakened by her father whenever he got up had lost its charm.

That wasn't the only difficulty of living at home. My parents stayed up to watch my reports on the news every night and were brutally honest about my appearance. More than once my mom or dad said something like, "That color you wore last night, that's not your best color. You should wear pink tomorrow." They also didn't hold back on commenting about my hair. They have always liked it on the shorter side. As a parent, I know they only want to be helpful, but the critiques didn't exactly thrill me. It was just time for me to move out and be on my own. Once I left for college, I spent very little time actually living in my parents' house. I had a couple of internships where I lived away from home and, as I mentioned before, I spent one summer living with my grandparents and one working as a waitress in Nantucket. I got used to my independence. My mom and dad wanted me to be self-sufficient. That's how they raised me. They wanted me to be able to make it on my own. When I asked if I could move back home for a while, they of course said yes, but I think they needed their space as much as I needed mine. I pretty quickly moved into an apartment with a friend from church and our other two closest friends lived directly across the hall from us.

Making it on my own proved to have a big learning curve. My initial salary sounded like plenty of money to a college student but I soon found out one of the hard realities of life as an adult: money doesn't go nearly as far as you think. Between paying rent, buying groceries and gas and clothes for work, I was barely getting by. I shopped sales and saved as much as I could but money was still tight. Some days I pulled up to the gas pump and put only $4.60 in my tank because that's all the money I had in the ashtray of my car, and half of that was change. More than once I had to call my mom and ask if she could float me a hundred-dollar loan to get me by until my next paycheck. I usually called after I bounced a check. Part of the money went to cover the bank's fees. I remember staring at my pay stub and shaking my head at the amount that had been deducted for taxes. If they'd just taken half that amount I wouldn't have had to ask my parents for any money, I thought. I'd worked all the way through college, so I knew all about state taxes, federal income tax, and Social Security. Now that I was making more money, the amount the government took seemed huge.

In spite of the struggles, I loved what I did. I was learning so much about the ins and outs of being a reporter. When you watch the news you see a reporter do a story that lasts a minute and a half or two minutes. What you do not see is how it took that reporter all day to produce those two minutes on air.

My days started with a meeting of the entire news team. We talked about what we wanted to cover that day. When news breaks, you obviously cover it, but a lot of the stories we discussed had been in the news for days. We discussed ways of going deeper and expanding the story with new information. That's why it's called the news. We want to give the viewers new information to keep them informed.

During our team meetings, we sat around a table and everyone pitched ideas. The news director then handed out assignments. He might tell me to go cover the escaped convict who was holed up in a nearby neighborhood or a local political controversy. I would immediately get on the phone and start researching the story and asking for on-camera interviews. If I could get one, two, or even three interviews lined up, I was good to go. My camera person and I then hit the ground running, crisscrossing the county trying hard to get our interviews and shoot the story quickly. The deadline was always looming. There was little time to even stop for lunch. We had to shoot our story, known in the business as a "package," and get back to the station to write the script and start editing. If I was assigned a story about politics, I raced to the statehouse, interviewed legislators, or anyone who was relevant to the story. I always carried legal pads to jot down notes since most people are camera-shy but are happy to give you all the details you want off-camera.

Once we got enough interviews and video, we went back to the station and I watched all of my interviews and wrote down everything the interviewees said. This took forever. I then sat down at my computer, wrote my script, and included sound bites from the interviews. Finally I was recorded reading my script and the editor edited his or her video over my voice recordings. For instance, if I was talking about a tax increase, the photographer added photos of people spending money.

I had to put my packages together quickly every day. The rule in journalism is: get your story on the air! My bosses didn't care if my equipment malfunctioned or if I had a hard time lining up interviews. In the newsroom you didn't complain. You just did as you were told and made your deadline. That left me always pressed for time. Meals had to be quick. Most days I only had time to swing by the Papa John's a block from the station for some breadsticks (with extra marinara sauce and no butter). I pretty much lived on this meal every day, but I didn't care. I was having so much fun trying to meet the challenge of hitting my deadlines.

Reporting in my hometown forced me to open my eyes to its problems and needs. I grew up in a nice home, with heat and only minor problems compared to many people in my city. I was covering stories in drug-infested neighborhoods and our homeless shelters. For the first time, I realized the world was a lot bigger and I was no longer seeing life in "Ainsley's world." I realized how grateful I needed to be. I was growing up and growing as a journalist.

Those first couple of years I learned a lot about writing, editing, and the nuts and bolts of broadcast journalism. The profession is stressful, the hours are crazy, there are so many demands and so much pressure, and the starting pay is not great. None of that mattered. I loved every minute of it. At the same time I stayed involved in my church, did a lot of Bible studies, and even led a Bible study for high school girls. Teaching them made me feel like I had a purpose and was making a difference. I also learned so much about myself and the Lord. I just wanted to get closer and closer to Him while also developing the talents He had given me.

# 6

## *Trying to Find My Balance*

Humble yourselves, therefore, under God's mighty hand, that he may lift you up in due time. Cast all your anxiety on him because he cares for you.

—1 PETER 5:6–7

I LOVED GROWING up in the South and will forever be grateful for the values and culture instilled in me. But as I have said, I knew God had something bigger planned for me. I know writing this makes me sound like I never grew beyond that five-year-old watching the Oscars and dreaming of becoming a famous Hollywood actress. Believe me, I've wrestled with that myself. After I became born again and began to seek God's will for my life, the sense that God had a bigger plan for me only grew stronger. Rather than make my head swell, I felt a huge load of responsibility. If God wanted to put me in a larger place with bigger responsibilities, I knew I had to be ready, both professionally and spiritually. I had to work hard to develop the talents He'd given me and to become the best I could possibly be as a journalist. At the same time I wanted to continue growing closer to Him, learning His word, the Bible, and becoming mature as a Christian. Learning how to balance the spiritual and the professional along with my social life and my love life and all the other parts of my life was a lot harder than I imagined.

The first couple of years I worked at WLTX I was a sponge, soaking up everything I could learn. During that time I covered everything from shootings to politics to hurricanes and natural disasters—whatever made news that day. I considered myself a serious reporter. Larry, my boss, also had me fill in as an anchor on the weekends, and I was eager for that experience as well.

But from the day I accepted my job I never planned on staying at WLTX forever. As I've said, ultimately, I hoped to land a job in a top-ten market, or move up to the national level, and I made no secret of that fact. When I dated someone, in the beginning I told him that if he wanted to be serious with me and move forward with the relationship, he needed to know I wasn't going to be in Columbia forever.

The boyfriend who drove me around to the different job interviews was Kevin. We ended up dating for five years off and on. We were both busy, trying to navigate our own paths, and were not sure if God wanted us to get married. We broke up several times and in between friends would set me up with other people. After a few dates, I would let them know I was not staying in Columbia because I knew God was pulling me in a different direction. I had the desire to try to get to the top and whoever I was going to end up with had to be okay with that. As expected, most guys were not. They wanted to stay in South Carolina and raise a family. So most relationships wouldn't last long because neither one of us shared the same goals. But I believed in being extremely honest and never played games.

TWO YEARS AFTER I started as a reporter, Larry Audas called me into his office and said, "I want you to be the new morning anchor."

"Me?" I asked.

"Yes, you. I want to pair you with Curtis Wilson. The two of you will make a great team." I did not know Curtis personally, but I was familiar with who he was. He had one of the most popular drive-time radio shows in Columbia. I'd listened to him. He was very entertaining, engaging, and funny.

"Larry, I look up to you and will do anything you ask of me, but I don't think I will be successful in that position. I am not funny and you need someone funny to fill that spot," I said. Morning anchors report the news but they also have to be entertaining. That's just not me. At least I didn't think it was me.

"Ainsley, trust me. I think you'd be really good at this," Larry said.

"I'm a reporter," I countered. "I do serious news. Besides, I stay up late. I like working the shift I do now. It fits me. Believe me. I am not a morning person. You do not want me on-camera at five A.M."

Larry just looked at me.

Long ago my father taught me that when you have a job, you do whatever work the boss throws your way. You don't say no to an assignment. "All right. If you want me to do this then I'll do it," I said.

"Good choice," Larry said. He later introduced me to Curtis. When Larry wasn't around I told Curtis all of my hesitations about taking the morning anchor position. It wasn't that I wasn't thrilled about working with him, I told him. I didn't know him, but from what I had heard on the radio I thought he was a great choice for the morning show. Me, that was another question entirely.

I should never have questioned Larry's judgment. Right from the start Curtis and I hit it off. The two of us on-camera just clicked. He quickly became one of my closest friends, and we still stay in touch. I love him like a brother. We had not worked together very long when Curtis told me, "I've worked with lots of personalities on the air over the years, and I'm telling you, this is your first anchor position but what we have is just . . . it's just very rare." I'm so glad Curtis told me this. Since then I've never taken my good relationships and chemistry with my co-anchors for granted.

Curtis brought my personality out on-camera. He taught me how to be Ainsley for all to see. I stopped pretending to be so serious all the time. In college and when I first started at WLTX I was under the impression that journalists could never be lighthearted. Curtis showed me that there is a time and a place for seriousness, but also a time and a place to have some fun. Our audience loved it. We soon became the number one morning news show in the Columbia market.

We covered serious topics on the morning show, but we also wove in fun, fluff news. Sometimes the fun got the best of us. I remember covering a story about a pig and Curtis and I couldn't keep our composure. A giant pig was essentially attacking a mobile home. That's right. Someone's giant-size pig escaped its pen and went on a rampage. A neighbor called the police and the media to report that her house was shaking because a pig was slamming its body into its walls. When a camera crew from our station arrived the pig was still at it. Curtis and I sat in the anchor chairs watching the video of the pig attack the house and it struck both of us as one of the funniest things we'd ever seen. Now, I was a serious news anchor, but I couldn't take this seriously. Curtis leaned over and began acting like he was clearing his throat to try to cover his laughter. He'd pull it together, then read another line of the story, and start clearing his throat again. I didn't even try to hide my laughter. About the time I got myself together I looked over at Curtis and I burst out laughing. That story helped me begin to loosen up on air and let more of myself come out.

Curtis was always trying to teach me not to take myself so seriously. I cannot count the number of times the camera moved in close on me as I reported a story while just off-camera Curtis raised up and put his face as close as he could to mine without showing up on-screen. He'd stare at me or jab me or do whatever he could to try to get me to laugh while I read the news. I'd pay him back when we cut to commercial. All he wanted to do was pull my personality out. Curtis knew, and Larry knew, that that's what connected us to our viewers. Yes, we needed to report the news and give stories the weight each one needed, but I truly believe we shot to the top of the ratings because of our personalities. The viewers watched because they felt connected to us. Curtis understood this from his drive-time radio show. I was just starting to learn it.

I finally cut loose completely and was just myself one morning when Curtis tried to embarrass me on-camera. Scott, our meteorologist, was doing the weather while I was not on-camera. I had a makeup bag about the size of a small cooler that I kept under the anchor desk. Since I was off-camera, I pulled out my bag and did a quick fix of my makeup. I didn't hear a word of Scott's weather report. After he was finished he tossed back to us and asked a question while I wasn't listening because I was hastily putting my makeup bag away. Still I said, "Oh yeah, yeah," like I'd been paying close attention to his every word.

"Uh-uh. No, no, no, no. You're not getting out of this one, Ainsley. Don't act like you were listening to Scott's forecast. You didn't hear a word he said, did you?" Curtis said.

"I did. I was listening!" I protested.

"Then what's the weather going to be today?" he asked.

"Curtis! Are you trying to get me in trouble?" I said with a smile.

Curtis then reached down and picked up my makeup bag. "This looks like a cooler. It looks like you have a six-pack of beer in here. Ladies and gentlemen, this is Ainsley's makeup bag. Ainsley, why don't you tell everybody what you were doing during Scott's weather report?"

I laughed. "Well, if you aren't quiet I'm going to put some of this makeup on you, Curtis," I said. "Oh, wait a minute. You're already wearing makeup. You're the only man in my life who wears makeup."

Curtis and I also made appearances all over the city. He had become deeply involved in the community through his radio program before he joined WLTX. Organizations all over the city asked him to appear and he always said yes. If a school asked him to come read to fourth graders, he said yes, and I went with him. If a nonprofit wanted him to come speak, he said yes, and I went with him. Curtis even said yes if a local kid was having a hard time and wanted Curtis to meet him at McDonald's or Hardee's. The man lived out his Christian talk. He was generous with his time and money and just wanted to help people.

It didn't take long for our schedule outside of the show to fill up. Since Curtis never said no, and he nearly always invited me to come along with him, I found we had an appearance of some sort nearly every day. I've always been very organized with my time. I have a physical month-to-month planner and rely on it heavily. I schedule my time down to the half hour. The more appearances I did with Curtis, the more the thirty-minute blocks on my calendar started to run together. I soon found myself overwhelmed. I felt like work was consuming my life. I finally went to Curtis and told him I had to step back. I agreed to do one or two appearances a week, but that was all. I had to bring balance back into my schedule. "I love being involved in the community and these are the people who put food on my table by watching our show, and I want to show them my appreciation, but I know what my limits are," I told him.

The problem wasn't that I had reached my limits on interacting with people. My life had fallen out of balance. I hardly had time for my family, boyfriend, or for the Bible study I led for a group of high school girls from my church. I needed to figure out how to get things back to where they belonged.

A LITTLE LESS than a year after I took the morning anchor position, Larry called me back into his office. "I need you to cover the Sanford election watch party and interview him after the results are in," he said to me. Mark Sanford was the 2002 Republican candidate for governor of South Carolina. I'd interviewed him on set as part of the morning show but that was very different from covering his campaign on its biggest night. During the campaign I'd also interviewed the Democratic incumbent, Jim Hodges. Governor Hodges appeared on our show many times during his term in office. He made himself available to the press more than any politician I've ever seen. I really appreciated that about him.

Even though I had interviewed both candidates in the governor's race, that did not make me comfortable covering politics. I'd even interviewed former president Jimmy Carter on the release of his book *An Hour Before Daylight: Memories of a Rural Boyhood*, but we didn't talk about his political views. My family didn't discuss politics when I was growing up. My father told us how important it is to vote, and my parents were very conservative, but I never heard them talking about candidates or issues. We spent our time around the dinner table talking about our days and whatever was going on in our lives.

I agreed to do the assignment since Earhardts don't turn down work assignments, but I was nervous. I had no idea what I should ask the possible governor-elect or how I should ask it. Looking back after working at Fox News for more than a decade, I find it funny that I felt so inadequate covering politics. Today I come up with questions in a heartbeat, but back then I agonized over every question I prepared.

On the night of the election I went to the local barbecue restaurant where the Sanford campaign was holding its watch party. We South Carolinians love our barbecue, so a candidate for governor holding his election-night party there did not seem at all out of the ordinary. At least I knew the food was going to be good, but I was almost too nervous to eat. When I arrived I spotted a friend's husband, Aaron, who was a reporter for a local paper. Aaron had covered political campaigns for years. I rushed over and pulled him aside. "Aaron, will you please look over these questions I've prepared for when I interview Mark Sanford once the results are in and let me know what you think?" Thankfully, he agreed. He gave me some advice and even suggested a couple more questions. I felt more prepared, but still nervous.

Early in the night I interviewed then-candidate Sanford but the questions I asked had been easy to come up with. He'd held a lead in the polls up to the election, so I asked him how he felt waiting for the results to come in. He answered exactly like any candidate answers those questions. I didn't expect anything different. Honestly, I had trouble containing my excitement at having a front-row seat for the election.

Finally the votes were in. Governor Hodges conceded the election. Everyone in the restaurant cheered and yelled. The new governor-elect came out and made a speech. Then it was my turn. To be honest, I do not remember anything I asked him. Once the interview was over, I let out a sigh of relief, did a couple of final reports for the late news, then headed home.

A couple of days after the election Larry called me into his office. "I need to give you some constructive criticism," he said. I knew I needed to hear what he had to say, but I dreaded it at the same time. I always wanted to do the best job possible. No one likes hearing they messed up.

"Okay," I said.

"You asked Sanford too many softball questions. I could tell you were excited about him winning. It was obvious you liked him as a candidate," he said.

"To be honest, Larry, I wanted to be nice to him because that's my nature and I've never really covered politics to that degree before. But, please tell me what I should have done differently."

"You need to ask tough questions but also be fair. As a journalist, you cannot be biased. You have to play both sides and treat both sides the same," Larry said.

Every time I now interview a politician from either major party I hear Larry's words echoing in my ears. Covering the Sanford campaign was a learning experience for me, just like nearly everything else I did at WLTX. Through the three years Curtis and I anchored the morning show I felt myself growing professionally, spiritually, and personally. Not only had I gained a better understanding of what it meant to be on camera every day, but I came to see what my responsibilities were as a journalist—both to viewers and to myself. Though it was still hard for me to be fully myself on camera, I knew it was something that I could continue to improve. It had been my dream job, only my dreams were bigger. When my contract came up in January of 2005, I decided to spread my wings and see where they might take me.

# 7

## *Ready for a New Challenge*

Go from your country, your people and your father's
household to the land I will show you.

—GENESIS 12:1

I COULD HAVE stayed in Columbia forever. My family was close
by, which allowed my parents and grandparents to watch me
anchor the morning news every day. The station steadily increased
my salary every year, which allowed me to move out of the apartment I shared with four other girls and buy a home of my own.
Curtis and I continued to top the morning news ratings. On top
of it all, Kevin and I decided to get married and we got engaged.
On a purely human level, I could have settled into Columbia and
spent the rest of my career and life there. We both went to college
there, had many friends in Columbia and both had good jobs.

But after five years at WLTX I knew it was time for me to
make a change. I needed new professional challenges. Aside from
my first two years of college at Florida State in Tallahassee and a
few summers living away from home, I'd never been completely on
my own. I may have owned my own home and had a burgeoning
career, but I remained close enough to my parents that if my old
Buick broke down, all I had to do was call my dad and he'd be
right there. It was time for me to strike out on my own.

The same was true of work. I loved WLTX and the people
with whom I worked, but it was my hometown station. I understood the market because I grew up there. I needed to test myself
by moving to a market that was not second nature to me.

My second contract at WLTX was ending, which made it the perfect time to see what else was out there. This was not a decision I took lightly. I prayed and prayed over what I should do. Proverbs 3:5–6 promises that God will direct my path if I trust in Him with *all* of my heart and lean not on my own understanding. That was my prayer throughout this time. I told God that I did not want Ainsley's way, but HIS way. I needed Him to direct me where He wanted me to be. The more I prayed this prayer, the more I felt my heart being drawn to Texas. I'd fallen in love with the state when I visited Dallas years before. I also liked the fact that it was westward. Texans are southwesterners. They are good people. They love God and America. I thought Texas would be a good place for a South Carolina girl to work before making the transition to either California or New York.

My agent at the time sent my tapes to multiple markets, including San Antonio, Texas. Not long after, I had offers from the latter as well as Chattanooga, Tennessee, and Little Rock, Arkansas. I ruled out Chattanooga after speaking to the news director on the phone and talking to different people who worked there. The station did not seem to be a good fit for me at the time. I flew out to Little Rock for a visit, and to be honest, I was not enthused at first. But, when I arrived I was pleasantly surprised with how much I liked the city, and the news director couldn't have been nicer. However, I was looking to step out of the box and find a new challenge and I felt like Little Rock would be more of the same. The news director wanted me to anchor the five o'clock newscast then eventually move up to be the main anchor (or so he said).

As a side-note, I have learned in this business that promises need to be in writing. And if they can't put it in writing when you sign your contract, there is a strong chance the promises will be broken. When I discussed potential jobs with my family, my parents always asked, "Did you get that in writing?" They had my best interest in mind. When I signed my first contract for my first job, my dad read it and said, "Ains, they own you." But, in my heart of hearts, I knew who owned me: God. He gave me confirmation after confirmation that He "had this" and I didn't need to worry. I didn't need any promises in writing. I knew God would get me where He wanted me to be using the tools He gave me: a positive attitude, a passion for my profession, a love for my bosses, and an excitement in being the "yes girl." I knew if I said yes to every opportunity, I would be considered a hard worker and an employee who was easy to work with. I prided myself on rarely ending up in the boss's office. I rarely called for a meeting (out of consideration for them) and always reminded myself that less is more. That is, the less I bugged and nagged my bosses about a better position, the more they would notice me.

Don't get me wrong. There is a time and a place for telling the bosses what you want. If you want a raise, ask for it. In October 2017, I interviewed Ivana Trump, President Trump's first wife. I found her to be an amazing mother and a strong woman. During our interview she told me the key to keeping her children out of trouble as they were growing up was to keep them busy. Get them involved in every sport and after-school classes. And then, when they are teenagers, make them work and pay them for what they do. She said her son Donald Trump Jr. was working every day and complained about his salary over and over again. When he finally asked his mom for a raise, she didn't hesitate. They negotiated a higher salary. He then said, "Mom, why didn't you give me this earlier when I was complaining?" She said, "Because, son, you never asked." That is one of the best lessons you can learn for the workplace. If you go to the boss's office, tell her (or him) what you want. She (or he) can't read your mind. But—and this is crucial— always remember to be thankful for the blessings you have and make sure the boss knows how grateful you are.

My freshman year, my college roommate's dad worked for Disney World, and I asked her what it was like. She said, "My father refuses to say anything negative about the company. He says nothing but praises because he appreciates Disney for putting food on our table every day." That is the attitude I wanted to adopt when I got my first "real" job. That is why I decided to visit Little Rock with a positive outlook. I wasn't too excited about taking a job there because it seemed like a horizontal move. I was already in a similar city. But it helped that the news director was offering more money than the station in Columbia. Even so, my expectations were low. What I discovered surprised me. Little Rock is such a wonderful, southern city. My potential news director took me to the best-known steak restaurant downtown and I had the best steak I had ever had. As a bonus, there was a live jazz band playing just outside the front doors for a public celebration. The downtown had a great vibe to it. By the time I flew back to Columbia I could see myself living in Little Rock. I thought I might have found my next job.

Then I flew to San Antonio.

Kurt Davis, the news director at KENS 5, met me at the airport. I went dressed for success. I wore a business suit on the plane and brought high heels (to throw on when we landed). I wanted to present the image of a serious newswoman. As the old adage says, "You never get a second chance to make a first impression." When I walked off the plane, ready to go, Kurt was there to greet me. He was casual, wearing jeans, and said, "We're going to dinner." I felt completely overdressed and uncomfortable. I decided in that moment to be myself and ask Kurt an honest question. "Do you mind if I zip into the ladies' room and change into some jeans too?"

"No, not at all," Kurt said. He loves that story and reminds me of it to this day. Later he told me that right then he knew he'd found his anchor.

Kurt took me to an Italian restaurant. As we talked about the job I noticed an Englebert Humperdinck song playing in the background. The song took me right back to my childhood. My grandparents (on my dad's side) loved his music. When I was a little girl they gave me a record player and a bunch of their old records. I played their old Englebert Humperdinck albums over and over. I enjoyed listening to his music when the house was quiet and everyone was asleep. Being up at night when everyone was sleeping was something I enjoyed (to this day I love "Ainsley Time"—time alone to just watch TV, read my Bible, write letters, or organize my closet). At the time I would listen to my music and feel like I had the house to myself. Back then, Ainsley Time was finishing an art project, spending hours flipping through fashion magazines, cleaning out drawers in my bedroom, or rearranging the furniture. So, when I happened to hear an Englebert Humperdinck song playing at this Italian restaurant, it took me back to a happy time. I felt like it was a small nudge from above telling me, "This is where you need to be." Now, I obviously didn't make my decision based purely on what song happened to be playing while I was eating dinner with the news director from a potential employer. Many other factors came into play. However, hearing this song in this setting immediately put me at ease. It made San Antonio seem a little more like home even though I'd only been there a few hours. I've found that God uses little things like this to reassure us that we are on the path He's laying out for us.

By the time I left San Antonio, I knew I was going to accept this job offer. My agent negotiated a contract for me that doubled what I was making at WLTX. The contract was for three years but we inserted a clause allowing me to leave after two if I got a job offer in a top-ten media market or a national news outlet or in Phoenix. The top-ten media markets include New York, Los Angeles, Chicago, Philadelphia, Dallas/Fort Worth, the San Francisco

Bay area, Washington, D.C., Houston, Boston, and Atlanta. While Phoenix is just outside that list, I included it because my grandmother Mimi loved the area and I was intrigued.

The bosses agreed to the opt-out clause. We had a deal in place. I wanted to always be aligned with God's will, but in my heart of hearts I didn't think I would stay in San Antonio forever. I wanted to end up in a bigger market.

Now came the hard part: telling my bosses at WLTX and saying good-bye to Curtis, my co-anchor, and all the friends I had made working there. Larry Audas was no longer the news director. He was still in the Gannett family, but he was moving up the ladder and taking advantage of new opportunities. Larry had done so much for me. He hired me right out of college. He believed in me and took a chance. Then, years later, he made me the morning and noon anchor, which helped prepare me for where I am today. God used WLTX as the foundation of my career.

When I told the bosses I was leaving they said, "What can we do to convince you to stay? Can we match the salary? We just don't want you to leave."

I was flattered and thankful, but I knew I needed a new challenge and I could find it in Texas.

EXACTLY FIVE YEARS after I started at WLTX I packed up all my belongings and moved twelve hundred miles west to San Antonio. In January 2005 I became the new morning and midday anchor at the CBS affiliate KENS 5. Four months later, Kevin and I got married back home in Columbia. The wedding took place at the First Presbyterian Church and the reception was close by at the governor's mansion. Because of the location, Governor Mark Sanford, whose campaign I had covered, was invited, but was unable to attend. Indeed, rather than the governor, it was the

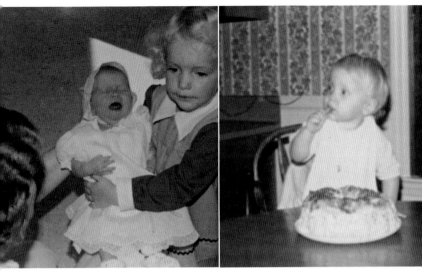

*Top left:* My sister, Elise, holding me for the first time in Mary Black Hospital in Spartanburg, South Carolina, where I was born in September 1976.

*Top right:* Celebrating my first birthday cake in 1977. Our family still has that highchair.

*Bottom left:* With Elise in the den of our Spartanburg home. The dog in the background was Puffin, our Peekapoo, who died at seventeen years old (my parents' first baby girl). The den was where I eventually would watch the Oscars and cry because I wanted to be there, and also where I would sneak in to watch soap operas with my nanny.

*Bottom right:* Elise and me at the beach in South Carolina.

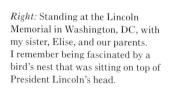

*Top:* Our first family trip to Washington, DC, standing in front of the White House. Little did I know that one day I would be inside the Oval Office interviewing the President.

*Left:* Taking in the sights in Washington, DC. My parents always instilled in us that reading about and understanding America were incredibly important.

*Right:* Standing at the Lincoln Memorial in Washington, DC, with my sister, Elise, and our parents. I remember being fascinated by a bird's nest that was sitting on top of President Lincoln's head.

*Top left:* Easter Sunday with my family in Spartanburg, South Carolina. God and the church were always big parts of our lives growing up, but it wasn't until later that I became more expressive about my faith (from left to right: Elise, me, Mom and Trent, Dad, and our dog, Puffin).

*Top right:* This photo was taken in our backyard in Spartanburg, South Carolina. It was a large backyard with honeysuckles and beautiful azalea bushes everywhere. Elise and I are holding hands with our younger cousin, Walker. We were the first three grandchildren and there are six total. My mom has three children and my aunt, Lynn, has three boys.

*Bottom left:* Christmas was always a special time in our house. This photo of Elise and me in our matching pjs was taken Christmas morning in our living room in Spartanburg.

*Bottom right:* Growing up, Elise and I were really close—especially when we started sharing a room after my brother, Trent, was born.

*Top:* My family with my dad's wonderful parents, Tinka and Lewie Earhardt, and their dog, P.G. We called our grandparents (on my dad's side) by their first names. Our friends got a kick out of that later.

*Bottom left:* My mother's parents, Ann (Mimi to me) and George (Pop to me) Giles. This was at my debutante ball in Greenville, South Carolina. They were members of the Carolinian Debutante Club and were so proud to present me that night, December 21, 1996. My grand-mothers were instrumental in helping me become the woman I am today.

*Bottom right:* My sweet grandparents (both graduates of the University of South Carolina) with our school's mascot, Cocky. They never missed a football game.

*Top:* Christmas Eve with my family in Columbia (From left to right: Mom, me, Elise, Trent, and Dad).

*Bottom:* At a family friend's house for my parents' annual Christmas supper club in Columbia, South Carolina. Once a year the children were invited to the adult supper club because Santa came to deliver toys at Christmas.

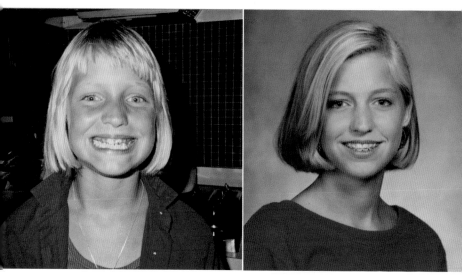

*Top left:* My interest in orthodontics started early. This photo was taken when I got my first set of braces in middle school.

*Top right:* This was my third set of braces (my teeth needed a lot of work) in ninth grade. I finally got my braces off a few weeks later.

*Bottom:* I was so proud when I made the cheerleading squad in seventh grade, but when I failed to make it in eighth grade, my father gave me advice that stayed with me for years to come: "God knew you could handle the rejection of not making the squad. He made you a confident, positive person. You will be fine."

*Left:* This shot of Trent and me was taken when we went to visit Elise, who was studying at Columbia College in Columbia, South Carolina.

*Above:* Visiting my grandparents at the Greenville Country Club.

*Left:* Winning Miss Congeniality in the Miss Spring Valley contest at my high school.

*Right:* My father presenting me on the football field for Spring Valley High School's Homecoming Court.

*Above:* My sorority initiation to Alpha Delta Pi at Florida State University in the fall of 1995.

*Right:* With my grandfather, George Wesley Giles, who presented me for the Carolinian Debutante Club at the Poinsett Club in Greenville, South Carolina, on December 21, 1996.

*Right:* My graduation from the University of South Carolina in 1999. While at the time the decision to transfer closer to home was a difficult one, looking back it's easy to see God's hand in the move. After all, it was the University of South Carolina's journalism school that set me on the path toward my passion.

*Above:* My dad and I sharing a moment after graduation from USC. Not only were there no more college tuition checks for my education, but I was his first child to graduate from his alma mater (my brother later did too).

*Right:* After graduation, I became the Richland County beat reporter for WLTX-News 19 in Columbia, South Carolina, which gave me a new perspective on my hometown.

*Top:* After finding success on the morning show in Columbia, I took aim at a bigger market and moved to San Antonio, Texas. This billboard was our San Antonio morning team in 2005 (from left to right: meteorologist Paul Mireles, me, my morning show cohost Fred Lozano, traffic reporter Megan Alexander). Paul is still at KENS-5 in San Antonio; Fred passed away at sixty-seven (bless his heart); and Megan, who remains a good friend, is a correspondent for *Inside Edition* in New York. We are currently in a Bible study together.

*Bottom:* When I was at WLTX-News 19 in Columbia, our crew traveled to New York for the Macy's Thanksgiving Day Parade and were on a float with Joe Torre, who was then the manager of the Yankees. We were covering a group of elementary school students from South Carolina, who had raised enough money to buy a new fire truck for one of the New York City fire houses after 9/11.

*Left:* Sitting on the set in San Antonio, Texas. I was the morning and noon anchor at KENS-5. I thoroughly enjoyed my time in San Antonio from 2005–2007. My coworkers, my friends, and the culture were wonderful. It was such a happy time in my life. But, I was always tempted by the prospect of a national audience, so when I got my shot with Fox News, I jumped right away.

*Above:* The day I signed my Fox News Channel contract. This was taken just before I left for the KENS-5 Christmas party in Texas. My boss announced at that party that I was leaving San Antonio to head to the Big Apple.

*Left:* This photo was taken on assignment at the Hoover Dam. I was a correspondent on Sean Hannity's show, called *Hannity's America*. I was the show's traveling correspondent and my weekly segment was called *Ainsley Across America*.

*Top:* One of the best days of my life: here I am with Will holding our daughter, Hayden DuBose Proctor, in the hospital on the day she was born, November 6, 2015.

*Bottom left:* Will and I honeymooned in France and London. We toured different regions and several champagne houses, including Moet and Chandon where Dom Perignon is made in Epernay, France. We bought a nice bottle of Dom Perignon for one specific reason. We would open it on the day our first child was born.

*Bottom right:* That bottle of Dom Perignon traveled with us from France to New York City and, after sitting in our apartment for years, was finally opened in New York-Presbyterian Hospital. The day Hayden was born we opened it for family and friends to have a taste and help us celebrate.

*Left:* Hayden with my parents the day after she was born. She was their first grandchild. *Photo by Brian Tully*

*Below:* Hayden on the day she was christened. *Photo by Brian Tully*

*Bottom:* With Hayden before a family meal during her baptism weekend.

*Left:* Sassy and Saks, my little loves. These "babies" came long before my daughter, Hayden. I was blessed with Sassy a few months after I moved to San Antonio, Texas. Saks joined our family shortly after and was a good playmate for his big sister, Sassy. Saks was only two pounds four ounces and is no longer with us because of health problems, but Sassy is still living up to her name at twelve years old.

*Right:* Hayden and I took this selfie before one of her classes. I thank God every day for her presence in our lives.

*Left:* Fox Fan Day at Yankee Stadium. Our staff gets to watch America's favorite game with our favorite people: our viewers. This was my first year at Fan Day hosting *Fox & Friends* and my daughter's first Yankee game. The team even gave Hayden a certificate to honor her first game. She was seven months old.

*Top:* My cohosts, Steve Doocy and Brian Kilmeade, and I interviewed President Trump at the White House in 2017, and afterward we took pictures in the Oval Office. *Official White House Photo by Shealah Craighead*

*Bottom left:* For Hayden's first Halloween, she was a ballerina. My husband and I took her trick-or-treating in our New York City neighborhood.

*Bottom right:* Anchoring *Fox & Friends* live from Philadelphia for the Democratic Convention in 2016.

*Right:* These are my "sisters." Our friendship dates back to the fourth grade at Windsor Elementary School in Columbia, South Carolina. We have been through ups and downs and had each other's backs always. Women need friends and God gave me two of the best.

*Left:* Many of the fantastic females in my family. My brother's wife, Darcy; my mom's sister, Lynn; my dad's brother's wife, Linda; my daughter, Hayden; my sister, Elise; my mom, Dale, and me. *Photo by Pasha Belman Photography*

*Right:* My family has been vacationing on Kiawah Island, South Carolina, since I was five years old. We have a small cottage there and have made many memories with friends and family. This photo was taken outside of the Sanctuary Resort where we went for dinner one summer night. (Dad, Mom, my sister, Elise, my husband, Will, me, my sister-in-law, Darcy, and my brother, Trent).

state police who showed up. They went straight to my father and informed him that they were going to shut the entire proceedings down because the music was too loud and a state ordinance required that all music be turned off at 10 P.M.

At first my father politely dismissed them because we had gotten special permission to play the music longer than the ordinance allowed from the Columbia police chief, who was there celebrating with us. Clearly, however, the governor and state law enforcement division carry more clout than the local police department. The state police threatened to arrest my father if he didn't comply. This time my dad listened. The music stopped and the reception ended earlier than any of us had planned . . . not unlike the marriage, unfortunately.

I continued to pray for God's will and San Antonio was where He called us. Kevin's and my first big decision involved buying a house. My mother always repeated the old real estate adage "location, location, location." She told me to buy the smallest house, or the most affordable house, in the nicest neighborhood. That's where we started looking. We toured homes in two historic, beautiful neighborhoods close to downtown and the famous River Walk. There wasn't much available in our price range. The only house that was a possibility was not in good shape. The building inspector found cracks in the foundation and other problems.

Since we couldn't find a house that fit us and our price range in the historic neighborhoods, we looked at a neighborhood called Stone Oak. It was on the northern side of San Antonio, where my boss, Kurt Davis, and his family lived. Our real estate agent showed us a brand-new home with three bedrooms, an office, and an open-plan living room/dining room/kitchen. The house also had a backyard for our dogs and all of the landscaping (including flowers) was taken care of by the homeowners' association. As we looked at the house the real estate agent added, "The neighborhood is called Stone Oak because 'all of the houses here are built on stone." My mind immediately went to Jesus' words from the Sermon on the Mount, where He says the wise man builds his house on a rock but a foolish man builds his house on sand. That settled it. The house was beautiful. No one had ever lived in it, which fit into my basic neat-freak nature. And it reminded me that for our home to last, we had to build it on the Rock, which is Jesus. We bought it and soon made it our home. Right after we moved in I took a rock out of the front yard and had Matthew 7:24 inscribed on it: "Therefore everyone who hears these words of mine and puts them into practice is like a wise man who built his house on the rock." We kept the rock in our house as a reminder of the true foundation on which a home must be built.

Working at KENS was a very different experience from WLTX because I was a different person. At my first job everything was brand-new, so expectations upon me were low. San Antonio was different, though. Here I came in as a young, but fairly seasoned anchor who'd left a top-rated show, which meant I had to be solid from the start. It helped that I sounded much more polished, the bosses at my South Carolina station having arranged for me to take voice lessons to help with my pronunciation and tone. When I worked in Columbia I sounded like everyone else because I was a native. But if I wanted to rise in my profession I needed to pronounce *pen* as *pen* not *pin*. And the number ten is not pronounced *tin* like the material once used to make cans. While you can never take all the southern out of a southern girl like me (thank goodness), I needed to learn to speak "properly" if I wanted to communicate with people outside of South Carolina.

Moving to Texas also meant leaving my family, but Kurt Davis, my new boss, made Kevin and me feel connected. On one of our early house-hunting trips, before I started the job, he took us to a Spurs game. That alone would have been amazing, but Kurt surprised us with court-side seats. KENS 5 was one of the team's biggest sponsors. The station had those two seats and a box for every game. One of the players on the opposing team had gone to high school with Kevin, and in the middle of the game, as the players ran past us, Kevin yelled out the name of his old teammate, who turned to us and said hey. We were beyond excited about the opportunity to move to San Antonio, and Kurt was smart to entice us as he had. He and the station manager, Bob McGann, were always so good about including us in life beyond the station. They took us to countless Spurs games, invited Kevin to play golf at some of the most exclusive clubs in the city, and treated us like family. We were always invited to their Christmas parties and to events like Tux and Tennies, a big fund-raiser hosted by the Spurs where the men wear tuxedos with tennis shoes and the women wear long dresses with tennis shoes. Someone from each table (KENS 5 always purchased a table) would go up onstage, reach their hand into a bowl, and draw a number. The Spurs player that wore that jersey number would come sit at your table and eat dinner with your group. We drew Manu Ginóbili. He was one of the best players on the team. He was also very cordial and polite, a perfect gentleman.

Professionally, KENS was good for me. Our morning and noon shows' ratings were rising, thanks be to God. I transferred my membership in the Junior League from Columbia to San Antonio and finished my provisional year. The Junior League is a service organization for women and was a wonderful way to meet others who had a heart for helping in the community. My mother and sister were members and I too wanted to be a part. I instantly met my closest friends in the organization, and as most wives do, we connected our husbands. Kevin and I started spending a lot of time with those other couples and became fast friends.

One of my friends, Stephanie Green, told me about her church,

Oak Hills. Kevin and I started visiting and fell in love with the preaching and music. The pastor, Max Lucado, is a best-selling Christian author and a wonderful teacher. Ironically, at the time he was a regular guest on *Fox & Friends*. This was well before I got a job in New York and a decade before I joined *Fox & Friends*. Today, when he comes on the show I am the one conducting the interview. That is wild to me!

Oak Hills was a wonderful church. It didn't have stained-glass windows or a long center aisle. Instead the facility was large and quite casual—there were no church pews, only folding chairs—but none of that mattered. Most important, I was "fed" there. The format was easy—we'd sing a few songs, listen to a sermon, and then have one more song. The contemporary music moved me, but Max's teachings were always Biblical and his lessons made me a better person. Having read many of his books, I liked his beliefs as well as his emphasis on family. Since it was such a large church, it offered Bible studies for all ages. Stephanie and I signed up for one together and met some wonderful Christian women. We prayed for each other, shared some of our deepest desires, discussed our unanswered prayers, and prayed for our city and country. We genuinely wanted to make this world a better place.

At work, I quickly settled in as well. My co-anchor, who has since passed away, was a strong but lovable man. He loved his children and talked fondly of his ex-wife (who used to be his morning-show cohost). They would take family trips together. I remember how proud he was to take all five of them (they had three children together) to Hawaii. I knew he was in a position to help and teach me, too, so I was constantly asking him questions about his life, living in San Antonio, the culture and how to even pronounce street names we had to talk about in the news. My goal was to immerse myself in the city and learn as much as I could, but more than that, I wanted him to respect me and know I was making an effort. The ratings continued to go up and eventually we became the number one morning show in San Antonio.

It was easy to enjoy life in San Antonio, and I was comfortable there from the start. The city and the job felt like the perfect fit. I loved my new house, my boss was great, my co-anchor and I worked well together, and Kevin and I had a fantastic circle of friends. San Antonio quickly became our home, and all in all, this could have been the end of my journey. But I knew my contract opened the door for me to leave after two years and my agent would be shopping me around. As that date drew closer I prayed for God's direction and wondered what He might have in store for me. I continued to pray for His will and had an open mind. Of course, a top-ten market would be a dream. As it turned out, God had something even bigger in mind.

# 8

## *Fox News Comes Calling*

Take delight in the Lord, and he will give you the desires of your heart.

—PSALM 37:4

T HE DAY BEFORE I turned thirty I was sitting on my back porch talking to my mother-in-law on the phone while my dogs, Sassy and Saks, chased each other around the yard. The call waiting beeped. I checked the caller ID then said to my mother-in-law, "I gotta go! This is my agent." She said something like, "Oh, wow, let me know what he says," then hung up.

I switched the line over and said, "Hello," to my agent, trying to sound calm.

"Are you sitting down?" he asked.

My heart skipped a beat. "Yes, I'm just outside with my dogs," I said.

"Fox News Channel called. They're interested in flying you in for an interview," he said.

I jumped up and said, "Are you kidding me?! THE Fox News Channel . . . that's the national level."

"Yes, Ainsley, Fox News Channel. They want to interview you. This is huge."

"Oh my goodness. National! One of the national news networks wants to interview me? Wow! When?" I asked.

"I have to work out all the details, but soon. Maybe this week," he said. We talked a little longer about the actual position for which I would be interviewed. I knew I was going to start out at

the bottom. Doing overnights was a possibility, as were other reporter positions. I would not know for sure what my duties would
be until they actually offered me a job. Even then I knew things
could change at any time.

As soon as I got off the phone, I called my husband, who de-
lightedly agreed this was the best birthday present ever, and then
my parents, who of course were equally thrilled. As soon as I hung
up, I started making arrangements for the trip. My agent called
back and told me that the interview was in two days. I scheduled
to take the day off work. Then I went shopping. If I was going to
interview for a national news channel I wanted to feel my best.
I found a black, knee-length pencil skirt that was a splurge for
me. I remember it cost more than a hundred dollars and I was a
T.J.Maxx and Marshalls shopper who was used to getting a nice
item at a discount. But I justified spending more on the skirt because the top combination was on sale. I wore a rust-colored tank
that had a matching little, short jacket with a ruffled edge. I loved
it. The ruffles flanked my neck and stood up like a collar. I wore
black, pointed high heels and felt professional and pretty in the
outfit. I kept it for a very long time because it represented a very
special time in my life.

Two days later I was on a direct flight from San Antonio to
Newark, New Jersey, which is just across the Hudson from Manhattan. Throughout the flight I felt such a sense of gratitude to
God. I spent much of my time going over the notes I had made
to prepare for my interview. I went over the names of those who
worked at Fox News and also reviewed what I wanted to get out
of the job. The pilot came over the loudspeaker and announced
we were starting our approach for a landing. The plane descended
and I could see the skyscrapers and the New York City skyline. I
stared out the window, tears streaming down my face. Whether I
got the job at Fox News or not, I felt so incredibly blessed by God

to even have this opportunity. Seven years earlier I was in the middle of my last semester of college, frantically putting together audition tapes and hoping to land a job somewhere. Now I was on the brink of moving to the national level in New York.

As the plane descended into the airport I wept and wrote a prayer in my journal, thanking God over and over for bringing me here and giving me such an incredible birthday present. *Father, I want your will to be done*, I prayed. *Show me if this is the right job for me. You and you alone hold the future in your hand. If you want me at Fox News I pray that you will pave a way before me and give me favor with the bosses at Fox News I will meet tomorrow. If not, make that just as clear. Open or close this door in an unmistakable way.* On a human level I really wanted this job but I also knew my Father in heaven knew what was best for me. I wanted His plan, His will, His best more than I wanted any specific job.

A car met me at the airport and took me to my hotel in midtown Manhattan not far from the Fox News Channel's building on Sixth Avenue. By the time I got to my room I was very hungry because I was so nervous that I hadn't eaten much over the past few days. I ordered a slice of New York pizza and a glass of wine through room service. Maybe it was because I was so hungry, but that slice of pizza was the best I'd ever had. While I ate I watched Fox News and reviewed my notes for my job interview the next day. I then crawled into bed and read my Bible and prayed. My agent told me to familiarize myself with the heavy hitters at Fox News. So I did my homework. I studied notes on all of the bosses just in case we crossed paths during the interview. I also looked over my résumé to make sure I was prepared to discuss any of my past experiences.

One part of my résumé made me a little nervous. Back in college I worked for South Carolina's junior United States Senator, Fritz Hollings. I sort of backed into the job. One of the girls in my sorority worked for him, but she had to give up the job the next semester because it conflicted with her schedule. When she asked if anyone wanted the job I immediately raised my hand. Since I planned on a career in journalism, I thought working for a senator would give me some great experience. I was right. I worked in his local South Carolina office answering the phone, helping constituents, opening mail, and clipping news articles I thought the senator might be interested in reading. Working for him taught me a lot about government, and the job paid well. However, when my conservative grandfather, Pop, found out I was working for a Democrat, he said to me in that grandfather tone of voice, "Honey, I wouldn't tell a soul." That story still makes me laugh.

I didn't hide the fact that I worked for a senator. It was right there on my résumé. However, I did not include the senator's name or party affiliation. It's not that I was ashamed of the work I did. I simply did not want anyone to prejudge me based on my former boss's politics. Now, all these years later, I hoped the question wouldn't come up in my Fox News interview for the same reason. Looking back over that line of my résumé, I decided that if the question did come up, I'd tell the story, including my grandfather's line, and leave it at that.

After going back over my résumé and trying to prepare for any question I might be asked, I tried to calm myself and get some sleep. Before turning out the light I called the front desk for a wake-up call, set the alarm on the alarm clock in the room, and gave myself plenty of time to get ready without being rushed.

The next morning I spent time alone with God in prayer then watched the news while I did my hair and makeup. I felt nervous but excited. I also felt very confident that whatever God wanted was going to happen. If He wanted me to have the job, I'd get it. If He didn't, then He'd make that clear as well. I knew I had to be as prepared as I possibly could be for whatever opportunity God had in mind. Some might mistake my surrender to the will of God as some kind of fatalism, where God's going to do what God is going to do no matter what I do. That is not a biblical idea. God has gifted each one of us with talents and abilities that He wants us to use for His glory. We must do everything we can to develop these gifts and then leave the results up to Him. That's how I felt when I walked out of my hotel on the morning of September 22, 2006. I had tried to be as prepared for this moment as I possibly could be. The rest was up to God.

I walked to the Fox News building from my hotel. I signed in and went through security. The officer directed me to the elevator bank and told me to go to the second floor. I found the elevator I needed to take but then I ran into a problem. There wasn't an "up" button. Instead there was a keypad. I had no idea what to do. As I stood staring at the keypad trying to figure out how to get to the second floor, Steve Doocy walked by. He looked up at me, smiled, and said hi. I was so impressed that one of the stars of the network was so friendly. I said hi back. He was the first on-air person I met at Fox News and now he is my co-anchor.

About that time someone else came over to the elevator. "Here, I'll help you," he said. "I know these are different, and if you aren't from New York, you've probably never seen them before." I think my lingering southern accent gave me away. He said, "What floor are you going to?"

I said, "The second floor." I watched as he pushed in the number 2 and waited. Then a letter popped on the screen directing me to the H elevator. I got on the elevator marked *H* and thanked the man for his help and went up to meet the Executive Vice President Head of Programming.

When I reached the second floor, a man was sitting behind the reception desk and he introduced himself as John. "He will be with you in just a minute," he said.

After what seemed like an eternity but was actually only a minute or two, the EVP's assistant came out and invited me to follow her into his office. I took a seat on a chair in front of his desk and he took a seat behind the desk. He introduced himself, and then the number two programming executive also came in. They talked to me about Fox News and what they were looking for in the next employee. The entire time I sat with them I continued praying, *Lord, give me the right words.* At the same time they didn't ask me what I thought they were going to ask. Because the interview did not go the way I had imagined it should, I kept thinking to myself, *You have blown it, Ainsley. You are not getting this job.*

Finally they asked if I would like to see the facility and, of course, I did. Everything kind of ran together in my mind, but I do remember standing with the EVP watching a live broadcast of Bill Hemmer anchoring the *America's Newsroom* show. Watching Bill took me right back to my days of working late nights in Columbia. I loved a show on CNN with Bill and Anderson Cooper. *Talk about full circle*, I thought.

At the end of the interview, I met with Roger Ailes in his corner office overlooking the Avenue of the Americas in midtown Manhattan. I looked out at the flags flying along the avenue and my mind raced back to all the movies I'd watched that were set in New York. So many showed scenes of Rockefeller Center or Sixth Avenue—right outside the window. Watching those movies, I used to envision myself walking down these streets, in a navy suit, my high heels clicking, and carrying my briefcase on my way to my corner office. Now here I was hoping to be in the building permanently. Across from me sat one of the most powerful men in television news. All I could think was, *How did I get here?* It had to be God.

Many allegations about Roger Ailes have come out in recent

years, allegations that led to his resignation from Fox News in July 2016. I was heartbroken when I heard the charges against him, but more than that, I was shocked. The man described in those charges was not the man I met that first day or the man I got to know at Fox News in the coming years. From the first day I met him, he was always a father figure and a mentor. But clearly that was not the experience other women had with him, and upon hearing their stories, my heart broke for them. I was shocked and saddened, but the man described in those charges was not the man I knew.

While the allegations against Roger rocked Fox News, we had no idea it was just the beginning of a wave of accusations that would sweep up men throughout media—from Hollywood figures like Harvey Weinstein to morning show presences like Matt Lauer. As a result, we've all had to struggle to reconcile these public figures with their private transgressions. This is especially true when we know the men being accused. At least, it was for me.

Of course, all this was years in the future during my first meeting with Roger Ailes, and nothing could have been further from my mind. Indeed that first meeting set the tone for our relationship the entire time I worked for him. He started off asking about me. He asked what my parents were like and how I got into this profession. He wanted to know who my heroes were and what my goals were. He also asked about my journey as a journalist and how I had come to live in San Antonio.

At the end of our half hour together I looked at him and said, "Roger, you are a legend in this profession and I will always be grateful for the time you are giving me. You are such a busy man and I can't thank you enough for just sitting down with ME. I don't know if you will hire me, but I just want you to know that if you do or if you do not, I know I will be in the place God wants me to be." Then I added, "And I hope it is here."

"I want to see your tape," Roger said. "If your tape is good, then I think I can find a place for you here."

"That would be wonderful, sir. Thank you," I said.

As I walked out all I could think was, *Wow, God, you are so good.* One minute I wasn't sure I was making a good impression and then the next minute I was walking out of the CEO's office feeling confident. I reminded myself to just give it to God and trust Him.

On my flight back to San Antonio I took out my journal and wrote:

*Dear Father, today goes down in history. I interviewed at Fox News today and had the time of my life. Thank you, thank you for the amazing opportunity. I met some of your most talented children, the best of the best, and I am honored. At the end of the day and at the end of my life my family is most important. You are my Father and that will never change. I am so grateful. Again, God, thank you. I love you and want to honor you. Please put me where you can use me the most. September 22, 2006.*

Now, if life were a movie, my phone would ring as soon as I walked into my home in San Antonio. Roger Ailes would be on the other end. "Ainsley, we want you to come work for us right away," he would say. But life, unlike a movie, doesn't happen in two hours. The waiting was difficult, but I was sustained by prayer.

In the meantime, the ABC affiliate station in Washington, D.C., contacted my agent about me. I flew out to Washington for multiple interviews with the news director, Bill Lord. The interviews went well and I thought D.C. could be a real possibility, but no offer came in. Instead I waited to hear back from Mr. Lord or Fox News or maybe someone someplace else entirely, and learn what God had in store for me.

September turned into October. My agent called Fox News and asked for an update. They told him that they really liked me but that they were still going through the interview process with other candidates. "We love Ainsley. She's still in the running. We just need a few more weeks," they said. A few weeks later my agent called again only to hear the same thing. I prayed and prayed for God's will to be done, but I wanted to know what that will was as soon as possible. My husband and I talked about which we'd prefer, New York or Washington. He preferred D.C., but was really fine with either as long as I didn't have to work weekends. I had anchored the weekend news briefly in Columbia while we were dating, and the hours put a strain on our relationship. The truth was that I didn't really have to go to either New York or Washington. I still had another year on my contract at KENS. The morning news show was number one in the market, which meant I could probably stay there as long as I wanted.

I was anxious to hear back from Fox News, but I was learning my first lesson about corporate America. The hiring process takes *forever*. Nothing ever happens quickly. I had to tell myself over and over, "Welcome to the big time, Ainsley, you small-town southern girl. This isn't Columbia anymore."

Finally, in November 2006, I heard back from Fox News. They made an offer and started contract negotiations with my agent. They wanted me to anchor the overnight news cut-ins. It was not a glamorous position but it was an opportunity to start out at the bottom with a national news network. I thought about my grandfather, Pop, who worked his way up from the bottling floor at Coca-Cola to become vice president of the Greenville plant. His experience taught me that where you start is not where you end up. If you want more, you have to work hard and wait for the opportunity from God. That's what I intended to do. I decided to take the job. I was still in consideration for the 5 P.M. anchor position in D.C. and I thought it was proper to call Bill Lord and tell him to take my name off the list. I was being scooped up by Fox News, yet grateful even to be considered in Washington. When I told Bill my decision he said, "I've now lost two women to Fox News." The other was Megyn Kelly.

The hardest part of making the move to Fox News was, once again, telling a boss I admired and enjoyed working for that I was moving on to a different news outlet. I worked out the contract details with Fox News right before Thanksgiving and I wanted to tell Kurt Davis, my news director, of my decision before he left for the holiday. I had a plan. I called him and said, "I have a cheese-cake for you and your family that I want to bring over for you to enjoy." Bad news is always delivered best with desserts.

"Ainsley, we're actually on the road right now on our way to Louisiana for the holiday. Just put the cheesecake in the freezer and we'll enjoy it at Christmas. You're sweet to do that," Kurt said. I had missed my opportunity to get this news off my chest because I wasn't going to "break up with him" over the phone. When I told him after Thanksgiving, he and the general manager, Bob Mc-Gann, took me out to dinner and tried to talk me out of my deci-sion. "Whatever they're paying you, we'll match it," Kurt said.

"It's not the money," I replied. "I feel like this is an opportunity I cannot pass up."

"But you'll be doing headlines overnight," Kurt said. He shook his head. "Are you sure you want to do this?" Even my co-anchor at the time had said something like he'd never take a job at the national level if he had to do overnights.

In spite of that, I told Kurt, "I've had the best experience here and you've been so good to me, but God has made it crystal clear to me that this is where I'm supposed to go and I am going to follow Him." I was certain it was the right course. Not only did I believe it was God's plan, but I had always wanted to live in New

York and work at the national level. Now I'd found my chance to do both at the same time. And, of course, I wanted to make more money and the offer was better than my current salary. Plus, it was just a quick, direct flight from New York to South Carolina to see family.

I left that dinner thinking about what they'd said about overnights. That didn't bother me. I was determined to work hard and work my way up. I knew God had big plans for me, and those plans were going to be realized in New York.

# 9

## *Back at the Bottom*

Who is going to harm you if you are eager to do good?

—I PETER 3:13

W HEN I TOOK the overnight reporter position at Fox News I never thought one year later I'd find myself staring out the door of a plane, twelve thousand feet above the ground, strapped to an army officer, and wearing a parachute.

I did my best to smile into the camera as I set up the report, but all I really wanted to do was get this over with and return to the ground. I realize that skydiving with the army's Golden Knights, one of the most elite skydiving teams in the world, would be a dream come true for many people. Not for me, at least not at the time. While I considered jumping with the team to be a great honor, and I was thrilled to show viewers the risks our military men and women take on a daily basis, I'd heard too many skydiving horror stories to feel comfortable. One of my mom's friends broke both of her ankles when she hit the ground on a tandem jump. I mentioned that to the army officer who put me through a day of training. He told me to pick up my feet and skid along the ground on landing. If I did that, I shouldn't come away with any broken bones. Still, I was nervous. I prayed for safety when I got into the plane and I kept praying as it climbed up to jump height.

When it came time to actually make the jump, First Sergeant Mike Elliott, the same man who did a tandem jump with President Bush 41, hooked me tightly to his harness. I was nervous and scared and just wanted to be back on the ground, but I knew I was in good hands. The man who made sure nothing happened to a president was going to make sure nothing happened to me. I just had to trust him and rest assured he knew what he was doing.

I never could have jumped out of that airplane on my own. My worries that my parachute wouldn't open or that I'd mess up the landing and break my ankles or my legs or both would have kept me as far from that open door as possible. But when Mike asked me if I was ready to jump, I felt safe with him—and with good reason: I reached the ground safely with no broken bones.

Those same feelings perfectly describe my move to New York and taking the job at Fox News. I never could have made it on my own. It was too risky. Yes, I was moving to the national level, but that didn't mean I was going to be successful. When I took the job, I hoped that I wouldn't be on overnights forever, but I had no assurances that the position would lead to a better one. For that matter, I had no assurances that my bosses at Fox News would want to keep me past my first contract. I also did not know how I'd fit into New York. I dreamed of living in New York someday, but I did not know how a southern girl from a state where everyone knows everyone (at least it feels that way) was going to adjust to the city that never sleeps.

Doing a tandem jump with the Golden Knights meant putting my faith completely in Mike Elliott. I had to trust that he would pull the cord at the right time and keep me safe. Moving to New York, I had to put my faith fully in God. I had to trust that He was the one who had brought me here and I had to believe He had a purpose and plan in doing so. I fully believed it was God who had given me this opportunity. Now it was up to me to make the most of it.

Even though I signed my contract with Fox News around Thanksgiving 2006, my contract at KENS did not allow me to leave until after the first of the year. Professionally, that felt like a long wait, but the time went by fast. I didn't have an opportunity to find an apartment before moving to New York. Thankfully, I found a temporary place to live for one month while looking for a long-term apartment. Friends told me that I'd probably fit in best on the Upper East Side, but finding a decent-sized place I could afford was easier said than done. The first time I saw how much it was going to cost to rent a place I wondered what I'd gotten myself into. Until I moved to the city I never realized how expensive Manhattan truly was, especially compared to Columbia and San Antonio. Eventually I found a small two-bedroom with one bath on the Upper East Side and a larger two-bedroom, one-bath apartment on the Upper West Side. Kevin and I wanted two bedrooms so that family and friends could come stay with us. I later realized that we were paying more so that others didn't have to pay for a hotel room. That was not the smartest move. We should have rented a one-bedroom and bought a pull-out sofa.

When I had to choose between the apartments, I was torn. I loved the Upper East Side and many people told me it was preppy and southerners usually fit in best there. So I called my husband and asked him to make the decision (based on pictures and videos I was sending him). He called his friend who lived in the city and asked him. The friend told us to take the bigger one and said we would be happy in either neighborhood.

*Bigger* is a relative term when it comes to New York apartments. The Upper West Side apartment could hold most of our good furniture, but it didn't come close to holding everything from our house in San Antonio. I had to give away a lot of my furniture and the rest we sent to South Carolina to put in storage. The cost of storage units in New York was astronomical. I did, though, take my favorite pieces, which included the first piece of furniture I ever bought.

When I was a child, my mother said she had always wanted a

"rice bed." These are tall, four-poster beds made out of mahogany with hand-carved rice stalks on each post. I was determined to have one one day and that day came when I got my first job at WLTX. The bed cost $5,000. I waited to buy it until it went on sale. The furniture store in my hometown had a 50-percent-off sale twice a year. My mother knew this and told me to wait. When I bought the bed, I had to finance it with a no-interest loan. The store agreed to let me pay a hundred dollars a month. I sent a check each month and learned a value lesson: patience. Fill your home with pieces that are beautiful and meaningful to you. I learned to buy one piece at a time and eventually have a home full of the items I cherished and loved. That "rice bed" is a piece that will belong to my daughter someday and will hopefully be passed on from generation to generation. It is special to me and will forever remind me of my precious mother. I will never part with it, until my daughter, Hayden, wants it. That bed was moved from Columbia to our guest room in San Antonio and into our guest room in New York. Wherever I am, that bed will always be there too.

My first apartment in New York wasn't just smaller than the houses I'd owned in South Carolina and Texas, it was also much darker. I learned in that apartment the importance of having a window in every room. We did not have one in the kitchen or bathroom. Plus, we were on the second floor. That meant we did not have a view of the city and we could hear every ambulance, fire truck, or police car in the middle of the night. Truth be told, the noise did not bother me because it was part of the New York experience. In a weird way, I liked it. But the apartment was definitely cramped.

Moreover, the colorful rugs and furniture—lots of red, navy, green, and yellow—were perfect for a southwestern Texas home, but way too busy in a small apartment in the city. My taste has since changed. My current apartment is decorated with soft colors.

I love whites, grays, and light blues. I love how New York has made me evolve. The city is big, noisy, and crowded. My apartment is just the opposite: small, calm, and clutter-free. I love the convenience of the city. The grocery store, bank, dry cleaners, shops, and gym are within a block or two. I still feel like a kid in a candy store when I am walking down the streets. When I first moved here I wondered if that feeling would fade, but after more than a decade in the city, it has not. The Manhattan life invigorates me.

On my first day at Fox News I had to spend the day with Human Resources signing paperwork and meeting with various employees to discuss health insurance and schedules. I got the keys to my office and a tour of the facility. At one point I walked through the newsroom and I heard a voice from a cubicle say, "Hey, Ainsley."

I turned and saw Shepard Smith. "Hey, Shepard," I said, more than a little shocked. I then added, "I can't believe you know who I am."

"Yes," he said. "Do you need any help moving?"

I remember laughing and saying, "No, no, I think we're okay." All I could think was, *I'm not exactly going to ask Shepard Smith, one of the top anchors at Fox News, to come over and help move my boxes!* But the gesture was so nice, and it was sincere. That pretty much set the tone for the way I was welcomed into the Fox News family. From the first day everyone made me feel like I belonged. Now I tease Shepard and ask him, "What would you have done if I had said, 'Yes, please show up tomorrow at six A.M.?'"

My first week on the job I received a call from the Wardrobe Department. "We want to meet with you and determine what your taste is and what your look is so that we can help you shop," the friendly lady said.

I was over the moon. On my first day at WLTX in Columbia I had felt like I'd gone to heaven when Larry Audas led me into the supply room and told me to pick out whatever I wanted. Now I was going to get to pick out an on-air wardrobe the same way. I could not wait. In the past, I bought all of my own clothes. I had to be frugal and find pretty pieces at discount stores or on sale. When I bought my clothes for work I usually shopped at T.J.Maxx or in the suit sections of mall department stores. I would wait until they had good sales and buy a few at a time. I thought my clothes were nice and they were always good enough for local news.

The head of our Wardrobe Department, Gwen Marder, who is a dear friend of mine, said, "Come on in. Let's pick out some clothes." Gwen guided me and helped me find pieces that were flattering and comfortable for my taste. I remember her showing me a cream suit with beautiful details on the sleeves. It was perfectly tailored and fit like a glove. She mixed and matched skirts and tops, and handed me a variety of colorful dresses. Each item was exquisite. "We'll have these taken to your office for you," she told me. I thanked her while trying to contain my excitement.

FOUR WEEKS AFTER starting at Fox News I finally moved out of my temporary apartment and into my first, real New York apartment. All of the furniture I could actually fit into the place arrived from Texas along with boxes and boxes of my belongings. Kevin and I were unpacking boxes and eating chicken sandwiches from a local restaurant when my phone rang. One of the regular anchors of *Fox & Friends Weekend* was off and they wanted me to fill in for her. Of course I said yes.

I immediately stopped unpacking and started getting ready. I got my hair colored, nails done, and was checking off all the boxes. Keep in mind, I am a planner. I have to be prepared. It was hard to put the unpacking on hold because I was craving order and was excited about seeing everything in its place. But I had to prioritize, and doing a good job on *Fox & Friends Weekend* was most important. Meanwhile, my husband started getting sick. It must have been the chicken sandwich. He definitely had food poisoning. I was trying to care for him, but was anxious about the show. The contrast wasn't lost on me. Here I was preparing for one of the best days of my life and he was experiencing one of his worst.

I can still remember the first show like it was yesterday. I felt a mix of excitement and nerves. There was so much to do, to plan and prepare. I needed to know the news stories backward and forward, I needed a smart, sophisticated outfit that made me feel comfortable, the hair to match the makeup. Time was running out. I was all over the place. I thought, *This is my big break*. And it actually was in many ways. More dreams were coming true.

I remember picking out a cream skirt, cream tank top, and cashmere, mint-green sweater that tied around the waist. I thought it was classy and beautiful. I studied my notes and prepared for my interviews the night before (this was the night my husband was sick with food poisoning and we were living in a sea of moving boxes stacked to the ceiling). The morning of the show our gifted hair and makeup department worked wonders and I was ready. I sat on the set, the stage manager counted us down, and the red light came on. And just like that . . . I was anchoring *Fox & Friends Weekend*—my first national news show. Oh, it felt good. I was a nervous wreck, but prayed through the entire show.

Anchoring my first national program took me back to the day I anchored my first local news show. When those lights came on I was reminded of the story of Jehoshaphat in 2 Chronicles 20. Jehoshaphat was weak and unprepared to fight Moab and Ammon. However, before the fighting began, God reminded him that this was His battle not Jehoshaphat's. 2 Chronicles 20:17 says, "You will not have to fight this battle. Take up your positions; stand firm and see the deliverance the LORD will give you, Judah and Jerusalem. Do not be afraid; do not be discouraged. Go out to face them tomorrow, and the LORD will be with you." The Lord did exactly what He promised and Jehoshaphat won the war.

I thought of that same story once again when I took my seat on the curvy couch to anchor *Fox & Friends Weekend*. Remembering God's promise allowed me to breathe and let God speak through me. At the end of the three-hour show we signed off and I said, "This was the best day of my life." I was so appreciative of the opportunity I had been given. But I had a long way to go.

Being asked to fill in so soon after I took the job at Fox News made me feel like I was going to move up quickly. Why else would they have me anchor unless those who hired me saw bigger things ahead for me? My superiors' overwhelmingly positive feedback after the show only seemed to confirm this. One of the morning-show producers shared with me a message on his phone from our boss, who gave me rave reviews. I will always appreciate him for showing me that message. Most producers would keep the boss's messages private. The positive feedback helped build my confidence. Keep in mind, I am a girl from South Carolina who had just arrived on the big stage—any confirmation from a boss was much appreciated. The experience taught me to always encourage others and try to keep in mind what they might be experiencing. New employees need positive reinforcement. I just knew that the overnight position was going to be a springboard to bigger and better things.

In the meantime I had a job to do. Most nights I arrived for work around seven and went straight to the twelfth floor and the hair and makeup department. I became fast friends with everyone who worked there. They told me stories about a few people in the business who had forgotten where they came from and turned into divas. I told one of them that if I ever became too big for my britches they had my permission to physically slap me back into reality. From the start I understood we were all one big family. I couldn't go on air without those working behind the scenes. We depended on each other and we were all equally important. Those in front of the camera became the face of the operation but that didn't make us any more vital than the writer who put the stories together or the hairdresser who got us ready to go out in front of the camera or the custodian who kept the place clean. Every team member is just as important as every other.

When I started out I truly was at the bottom of the totem pole, but no one made me feel that way. Most days when I went into hair and makeup, one of Fox News's biggest stars, Sean Hannity, was also there getting ready for his show. At first I was more than a little in awe. Back in Texas, I'd watched his show every night before going to bed. But, like Shepard Smith, Sean came up to me and introduced himself. Over the next few weeks we'd talk while sitting in the hair and makeup room together. He always asked about how I was adjusting to the city and if my husband and I had done anything fun the past weekend. We had a lot in common and he occasionally invited us out to his home. I couldn't believe I was mingling with the Hannitys. They could not have been nicer and I was trying to play it cool, but I was new to the scene and Sean was a major celebrity. However, I learned quickly that he was just like us. He was normal and very down-to-earth. He didn't see himself as a celebrity. He was just trying to raise his kids, have a private life, and work hard.

In the years since, Sean has become a good friend. No matter if you disagree with his political views, he is a generous man who would give anyone the shirt off his back. He didn't grow up with much, so he appreciates everyone who has had a hand in getting him where he is today and he is always blessing others.

One evening, not long after I started at Fox News, I was in the hair and makeup room when Sean asked me a question that would set my career trajectory at Fox News. He asked me if I'd ever want to do some reporting for his show. Of course I said yes. A short time later I did my first report for him and it went well. The ratings proved it and that meant more opportunities to come. Although I was getting positive feedback at Fox News and from most viewers, the negative criticisms stood out the most.

I was not prepared. The national level meant more exposure and that meant more reaction from viewers. Good or bad. Not every viewer loved me in Columbia and San Antonio, but the negative comments were not loud. At the national level they were, and at the time I had thin skin. People posted comments on social media and blasted me for the smallest thing—a comment I made, a hair out of place, an outfit they didn't like, or the wrong shade of lipstick. I wanted people to like me, and when I started reading the hurtful, hateful comments it really bothered me.

One evening I walked into hair and makeup and Sean was there. "What's wrong?" he asked.

"Oh my gosh, Sean. I'm under fire for this and for this and for this." After working at Fox News for more than a decade, I now realize that coming under fire on social media is part of the job. Back then it was a completely new experience and it bothered me.

"Ainsley, Google my name," he said with a smile. "The first thing that comes up is 'Sean Hannity is a moron.'"

We both laughed.

"All these people may think I'm a moron but my ratings are good and I'm doing very well. Let them write whatever they want to write. I don't care. I am who I am and I'm not going to be someone different," he said.

That helped. "Thanks, Sean," I said.

Then he added a piece of advice I have never forgotten. "Those people don't know you," he said. "So why do you care what they think?"

Sean was right. As I got to know him and his family on a more personal basis I realized that they had a small circle of friends that they hung out with and listened to. He knew everyone was not going to like him and he didn't let it bother him.

With encouragement like this, working at Fox News became everything I'd prayed it would be and more. Every day I felt an overwhelming sense of gratitude to God for calling me into this business and opening this door for me. I think it is so important to express that kind of thanks to God, not only in our prayers but also in words we will remember. That is why during my quiet time early one Saturday morning I wrote the following in my journal:

*December 1, 2007*

*I've been in New York for almost one year. "From the fullness of his grace we've all received one blessing after another," John 1:16. I just watched a special about the life of Ruth Bell Graham, the wife of Billy Graham. I want to be like her, Jesus. And she and I both want to be like you. Thank you for being an example and sending such an amazing child [Ruth Graham] to follow you. She lived an extraordinary life because her only request was to live in your example. I want to be sharpened and always reminded that serving you is my one and only purpose on earth. I love you. You are my Savior, my leader, my Jesus. All days I want to praise you. I want to love you and please you. Forgive me if that hasn't been the case. Forgive my sins— the way I talk to my husband, the thoughts that enter my mind, the things that I do and say, losing my patience and being lazy, not witnessing, spending money, being materialistic, and trying to be the center instead of letting you get the glory. Father, let me be a good child. Teach me to represent your family well. That means building up my husband and loving him unconditionally. I'm so grateful that you have—time after time—blessed my life. I have lived all over, attended great churches, have worked on air in my hometown and at the national level now. I am fortunate. But if it all disappeared tomorrow I would be content because no one can take away the one thing I value most and that is my relationship with you. Daily I let others down, and vice versa, but you are forever steady, never changing, always there.*

Tears welled up in my eyes as I wrote those words. Jesus felt so close in that moment. I sensed His love washing over me and filling the room. I meant what I prayed. If He did take everything away, I would be content because the only thing I really need, the only thing I really want, is more of Him.

It is interesting to think (when we pray prayers like that) we never expect God will really allow the things we love to disappear. The real test of our faith comes when He does. It certainly did for me.

# 10

## *The Hardest Part*

Wait for the Lord; be strong and take heart and wait
for the Lord.

—PSALM 27:14

I DON'T LIKE to wait. That is not to say I am an impatient person. I don't lose my cool if the line is extra long at the grocery
store or if the barista takes longer than I expected to prepare my
drink. Becoming upset over such trivial things doesn't please God
and it is a poor reflection on me. When it comes to my day-to-day
life, I strive to show the fruit of the Spirit, which is patience.

But I still don't like to wait.

Sure, I can wait for my coffee, but when it comes to my career
and my goals, I hate it. From the day I transferred to the University of South Carolina, I had a plan for where I wanted to go in
life and I wanted to get there as fast as I could. For ten remarkable years everything pretty much went according to that plan. I
landed a great job right out of college in my hometown. Within
two years I received a promotion and a nice-size raise. Not long
after that the morning show I co-anchored hit number one in the
ratings and stayed there. Five years after graduating from college
I landed my second anchor position in a bigger market for more
pay. Two years into a three-year contract in that job, I made the
jump to a national news network; only, the move to Fox News
was not the end of my journey, more like the end of the beginning.
My goal was to keep moving up the ladder and land an anchor

position on one of the network's main shows. After that, only God knew what He had in store for me.

As I write all this it strikes me how overconfident I must sound. Believe me when I say that is not my intent. In my adult years, my goal was never to become famous or make a name for myself. I believe God gave me the abilities and the calling to be a television host, but all I wanted was to be was in His will. This job is His plan for my life. With that said, I did want to go as far as I could in my profession. I wanted to push myself, always work to improve myself, and become the very best I could be. I also believed that if I did that, the sky was the limit. I think this should be everyone's personal goal. God is not honored if we shrink back and fail to make the most of every gift He has given us. Making the most of His gifts must not blind us to all He wants to do through the journey.

Along the way I tried to always remind myself to soak up every experience, to be a good person and let His light shine as bright as possible. I also tried to do the one thing I now tell everyone just entering the business: Enjoy the ride. I did do that for the most part, but I would be lying if I didn't tell you I struggled at times. My Bible study in Texas at Max Lucado's church prayed for me to get the job in New York (after I flew up to Fox News for the interview). Years later, my Bible study in New York prayed for a new shift for me (I had the overnight shift at Fox News for seven years). Some believe it's selfish to pray that specifically, but I believe God cares about all aspects of our lives just like I care about my daughter's and want to know all of her hopes, fears, and desires.

I was incredibly fortunate. My journey at Fox News was just beginning, but I became the first person to be called if our female weekend anchor took the day off. Occasionally I also filled in for the female anchor on *Fox & Friends* during the week. I was learning a lot and enjoying the opportunities. I knew the bosses were testing me, and if I did my very best more opportunities would come. And they did.

At the same time my "reporting" for Hannity's show quickly became more than doing an occasional piece. When Sean initially asked me to report for him, he was cohosting his weeknight show with Alan Colmes, but was getting his own show on Sunday nights called *Hannity's America*. He and his staff created my own segment: "Ainsley Across America." The graphics department created a map of the United States with me in a convertible driving all over the country and waving to the folks. It was adorable and always put a smile on my face. I covered stories all over the country and learned so much about our communities and cultures and met amazing people. I jumped out of airplanes, flew in a fighter jet, covered the drought in the San Joaquin Valley, flew in a helicopter over the fields where most of America's almonds are grown, found myself walking in the Mojave Desert, covered spring break in Panama City Beach, Florida (our series led to spring break shutting down there. The bar owners hated us, but the residents and law enforcement cheered us on and still credit Sean Hannity for making Panama Beach safer). At the same time I was still working my overnight shifts, often filling in on *Fox & Friends Weekend*, and on my days off I traveled for Sean's show.

I hardly had a moment to call my own, but I did not mind. Working on Sean's show, I got positive feedback from his senior staffers, and their words fueled me, helping to build my confidence. A year earlier I'd been watching Sean in Texas; fast-forward twelve months and I was ON his show. God is good! This was another confirmation from the Lord. He put me in the path of yet another powerful, good person who wanted me to succeed.

After working at Fox News for a little more than a year, I learned *Fox & Friends Weekend* was about to go through some changes. The weekend female anchor moved to weekdays. That meant the weekend position was open. I started filling in one weekend after another. However, I was never named the formal replacement. I had to wait until the schedule was posted, on Wednesday or Thursday, to learn if I was going to be on the show that weekend. The uncertainty put my life on hold. I couldn't make weekend plans or go out of town because I wanted to be available to anchor.

The overnight staff was pulling for me. The overnight team was a tight group, in part because we were all so young but also because we worked tough hours in hopes of getting to the next level. When the weekend schedule was posted, the whole team was excited for me if my name was listed as the weekend host.

Very quickly I was filling in nearly every weekend. At this point I was working overnights Monday, Tuesday, and Wednesday, traveling for *Hannity's America* on Thursdays and Fridays, and then coming back to New York in time to anchor the weekend morning shows.

If *Hannity's America* asked me to fly to California, I flew to California on Thursday. If they needed me to jump out of an airplane in North Carolina with the Golden Knights, I did it on a Thursday or a Friday morning. I did whatever they needed me to do. I was constantly rearranging my life to accommodate my work schedule. I rarely had a day off and my sleep schedule was different each day. It was exhausting and grueling, but also invigorating. I felt needed at work and was continuously getting reinforcement from my colleagues. I prayed I'd be named the permanent female anchor of *Fox & Friends Weekend*. Every weekend I filled in was a working audition. I knew I had to prove myself.

I never said no to opportunities at work. Fox News never forced me to cover any stories, but because I always said yes, they kept asking. I tell journalism students that hard work is the only way to get to the top. There is no other way. That's why you must choose a path that makes you happy. When you work hard at a job you love, it doesn't feel like work. For me, every time I got an assignment that took me all over the country, I felt a rush of excitement. I also knew the story had to be covered. If I said no, someone else would say yes and get the opportunity. This was not about Fox News, this was about me and doing what it took to get my dream job.

Because my schedule ran week to week I could not make any plans. Weeks of filling the anchor position on *Fox & Friends Weekend* turned into months. I was exhausted but I kept pushing myself. Deep down I believed that there was no way they were going to have me fill this position for all this time and not offer the job to me permanently. And if they did I would finally be able to stop and breathe both personally and financially. Unfortunately, nothing happens quickly in this business. Contracts, personalities, and ratings are all involved. For all I knew, Fox News was waiting to see how the ratings on *Fox & Friends Weekend* were going to shake out with me on the curvy couch. That takes time. I learned in local news that it takes two years before viewers start recognizing the anchors. While I was eating, breathing, and sleeping the business, most people watching at home, especially for the weekend show, would tune in one week but be off on vacation the next and never turn their television on. It takes a while for the network to figure out a combination that's going to work long term with viewers.

I also had some work to do on how I was broadcasting. Around this time, I got some feedback that I needed to be more comfortable, more myself on camera. That surprised me because I thought I *was* being myself. The more I thought about it though, the more I understood the truth to the feedback. It was hard not to worry about what others would say or how I would come across. The problem was that I wasn't sure if I was ever going to be able to loosen up on television to that degree. I wanted the audience to see Christ in me and wasn't sure if I should open up. Eventually I would get to a place in my career where I was able to do that, but I wasn't there yet. I had work to do.

In the end, I didn't get the position on *Fox & Friends Weekend*. It was an incredibly difficult blow, especially because now there was no end in sight, no rest ahead. I had to keep pushing and pushing and working and working. I didn't know how much more I had in me. The days after I did not get the job were quite difficult for me, but they were also crucial for my growth as a child of God. I had been waiting on Fox News executives to make up their minds, but I was reminded that I am not supposed to wait on my employer or anyone else. As a child of God, I am to wait upon the Lord. He is the only one who can see my future. If God changes the direction of my life, He has a reason. Maybe He knew I wasn't ready and I was going to fail. Maybe He wanted me to hold on a little longer so that He could bless me with a different position (which is what happened). I didn't know the reason, but I trusted Him and kept surrendering all to Him.

I spent the next few days in prayer, leaning on the Lord. I found the strength in Him that allowed me to go in to work on Monday and keep doing the job God had given me. My coworkers were so supportive. They all encouraged me and let me know they were thinking of me as I went through this trial. Their encouragement helped. But what helped the most was my relationship with the Lord. I was so tired and I needed Him more than ever. I felt like I was falling at His feet and He was picking me up and carrying me, telling me to trust Him. Psalm 27:14 says, "Wait for the Lord; be strong and take heart and wait for the Lord." That's what I had to do.

The lessons I learned through this waiting were crucial as they gave me the strength to persevere through these challenges at work. But as it turned out they would become even more important in the months ahead, preparing me for a storm I never thought I'd face.

# II

## *Someplace I Never Thought I Would Be*

> The Lord gave and the Lord has taken away; may the
> name of the Lord be praised.
>
> —JOB 1:21B

THE DAY I got engaged to Kevin, one of my dearest, oldest, and closest friends, Cindy, gave me a new journal. On the first two pages I wrote out Proverbs 31:10–31, which was followed by this prayer:

*Jesus, the wife of noble character is exactly who I want to be. I promise to do my best to live up to those standards as a wife. I pray that my husband calls me blessed because of the love that I give him. I pray that we have healthy, beautiful lives. Smart, Christian children. I pray we as parents are the best influences that we can be. I pray for your grace and that I can be a wife who loves a lot, laughs often, and is full of grace. I want to be the most outstanding wife. I pray that through experience, prayer, Scripture, other Godly women, and a blessed marriage, you teach me how to be a wonderful wife. I also pray that this journal is a path into my heart. I pray that I journal our engagement experiences and cherish these always. Please be with me, make us loving and secure and teach us to live for you and not ourselves. Thank you for blessing me with great parents, a wonderful grandmother, and my grandparents who are already with you, Mimi, Pop, and Lewie. Thank*

*you, of course, for a God-fearing fiancé and his family. I
love you and I pray for peace. Love, Ainsley.*

About six years later I penned another journal entry, one I never
thought I would write:

*God, today my husband and I had a tough talk. My heart
was broken. He explained honestly why he hasn't given
his heart to me completely . . . I'm devastated. It was very
hard to hear because he was telling me that he doesn't love
me the way he once did. All this time I have been wrong.
I thought our love was mutual. I didn't think he could
survive without me. In reality, it's the other way around.
He will be fine without me and at the same time I'm glad
he was honest. This explains why he's not romantic. I pray
those feelings will come back to him. I pray you will change
his love for me and make it stronger. If not, I pray that you
will take care of me and watch over me. Please don't let us
have a family until his love for me is faithful, never failing,
and true. Thank you, Lord. Although today was painful
I know that I am one step closer to you and for that I am
grateful. Your daughter, Ainsley.*

They were hard words to write. Even now, all these years later,
looking back over them reminds me of the dark place I was in
then. As God would soon show me, it was of course all part of His
plan. But it would take time before I could understand it—and I
had to go through plenty of darkness to get there.

In truth, that journal entry had been coming for a while. Ever
since my work schedule had begun to consume my weekends,
things had grown increasingly difficult for Kevin and me. For
years, during football season, my husband and I would fly back to

South Carolina to see the Gamecocks play on the weekends. We had a parking spot for tailgating next to all of our closest friends and great season tickets. But once my work schedule at Fox News took over my weekends, Kevin began going without me, and the distance exacerbated the strain on our marriage.

It wasn't just football, of course—part of the problem was that my time was rarely my own. I remember being in New York working during Thanksgiving and Kevin decided to go home to South Carolina without me. Granted, I gave him permission to do it, but that didn't make being alone on the holiday any easier. I remember looking out of our apartment windows, talking to my family on the phone (as they celebrated together back home), and feeling so alone on that holiday. It felt like a normal day in New York, but I knew families all over the country were celebrating together, including everyone I loved. I reminded myself there would be many more Thanksgivings and sacrificing one for my family's future was worth it. Plus, anchoring on the holidays was always a fun experience. The shows are jam-packed with festivities and positive pieces. But once the show was over I was still all by myself in an empty apartment.

Over time moments like these took their toll on both Kevin and me. By the time we had the conversation that I wrote about in the journal, it had grown difficult to salvage the relationship. We were going in different directions, but also there were some trust issues I couldn't get past. Six months later we separated permanently. The following March the judge signed the divorce decree, and just like that, it was over. A signature made it permanent and final. In a way the divorce had been a long time coming, yet it was over in a heartbeat.

When I had walked down the aisle and recited my vows to God, I assumed our marriage would last forever. I committed myself to my husband, and more than that, I committed myself to the Lord. I fought to make the marriage last, and I was so angry at Kevin for not fighting and just letting me go. But things had happened that eroded the trust that is essential for any marriage to survive. Once that was gone, there was no hope of saving anything. It was heartbreaking and sad, but when the end came, I was ready to move forward.

Of course, as much as I could understand why the relationship had to end, divorce, for me, felt like another failure. Kevin was the first man I had truly loved and I was worried I would never feel that again. I had a hole in my heart and a pit in my stomach. Other people who had gone through the same experience told me it would take about five years to heal completely. I had dated Kevin for five years, was married for five, and now I had to go through the anger and grief for five more years? I wasn't sure I had the strength. Still, I remember my mom telling me that some people go their entire lives without finding love, and I was grateful I experienced it briefly.

Rather than giving up on life, I chose to look ahead and fight for my future. I once heard someone say that the present is a present. It's a gift from God. That's where I chose to live. You cannot look back on your past and ask yourself "what if?" and beat yourself up for not making different decisions. When it comes to my first marriage I can honestly say that I did my best. I did my best to be a great wife. That's all anyone can ask of themselves. I wrote out a list of all the things I wanted to do differently if I ever fell in love again. I didn't want to make the same mistakes and didn't want to compromise. I knew what I needed in a marriage and I actually knew myself better than ever.

On December 1, 2007, when I thought my marriage was strong, I wrote a journal entry (shared in chapter 9), and at the end of the entry I wrote, "But if it all disappeared tomorrow I would be content because no one can take away the one thing I value most and that is my relationship with you." With the divorce "all" had not disappeared, but a huge part of my life, a huge part of me, had. Now I had to choose what I was going to do. I had always chosen to look forward, but that wasn't the only decision I had to make. Every person who goes through a life-shaking trial must decide how the pain they experience will impact their relationship with God. It is easy to love God when life is good, but when things get hard, what then? For years I'd walked from one blessing to another. Now my life was taking turns I did not expect and did not want it to take. I had to choose how I would respond.

To me, there was only one answer. When my marriage fell apart and my career did not go as I wanted, I found God was the only One I could truly rely upon. When others let me down, I knew He never would.

The day I moved into my new apartment, completely on my own after the separation, I wrote another journal entry:

*Today is the beginning of a new life. I have packed up all my boxes and the movers just arrived. Not taking much with me but see this more as an advantage, a chance to start fresh. First, I look to you, Lord. Please be with me on my new journey. Guide my path. Help me make wise decisions and follow you every step of the way. Please be with Kevin and heal him of hurt, anger, and bitterness. Give us both peace as we try to figure out what is best for our lives. Psalm 124: "Be strong, take heart all you who hope in the Lord." Proverbs 16:3: "Commit to the Lord whatever you do and your plans will succeed." Today is June 2, 2009.*

The divorce was something I never wanted, but when it came, I knew that I was going to be all right because my God was never going to leave me or forsake me. I shed so many tears and had so many difficult days through the midst of it, but I was never alone. My Father was there, holding me. He was faithful. He always is.

I had no way of knowing it then, but the divorce was just one part of what would be my most amazing year yet, a year that showed me who I really was, and what God really had in store for me. My Jesus year.

# 12

# *Beauty from Ashes*

Be strong and take heart, all you who hope in the
Lord.

—PSALM 31:24

God,
*It is September 19, 2010, 10:41 P.M. This means I only have
a little more than an hour remaining in my Jesus year.
Your son died at thirty-three years old and my thirty-third
year has been my favorite thus far. Thank you for making
each year better. A lot has happened. Let's reminisce.*

*The big one. My divorce was finalized. At times the pain
has become easier and less frequent, I am so grateful. Once
again, you made my wrong right.*

*I have had a lot of fun going on dates with nice
gentlemen.*

*I went to Paris and I went to L.A. Both were on my
bucket list.*

*My brother got engaged.*

*Overall great, big, fabulous life full of dreams coming
true. Love, happiness, joy, and hope for even more. You
have blessed me, God, more than I could have ever believed
was possible. Thank you. I am sad a little because the
weekend is over. The friends have gone home. The birthday
party is over. It went by so quickly.*

*Now let's talk about my career. First, it's been an*

*exciting ride. To be on national television is a dream. Now I pray God please allow me to be a part of a show where I can show my personality and have fun. Please give me a chance—if you think that's what's best. Okay, I'm writing this and I'm realizing that I have been praying the wrong way. God, only you can see the future. Only you know what will happen, what is best for me and up ahead. Therefore, it should be so easy to pray about my career. Forgive me for my fear, unbelief, and selfishness. I pray that based on your knowledge, you will put me where you want me. Put me where YOU want me. Help me to be content and joyful right here at Fox News on the overnight shift. Thank you for giving me exactly what I need at this perfect, right time. I trust you and I give you my life and my future.*

*Now it is 11:07. I have fifty-three minutes left in my thirty-third year, my Jesus year. I have a great life, I have a lot of fun, and I love loving you, God. It's been the biggest joy and most rewarding experience out of every year, hour, or moment. What a journey. I love you and thank you. Can't wait to tell you in person one day.*

I WROTE THE above in my journal during the final hour of my thirty-third year. As it says, the year had been amazing, the best year of my life. However, it didn't start out that way. My "Jesus year" started with the cold, hard reality that my marriage was over. We tried to salvage it, but in the summer of 2009 I knew the damage that had been done was terminal. When I moved into my own apartment and the divorce was final, I did my best to be positive and look ahead. However, no matter how positive and forward-looking you may be, divorce exacts a toll on you.

At least it did on me.

The months of uncertainty left me exhausted. I had a deep,

empty feeling in the pit of my stomach that would not go away. There were days when I nearly doubled over from it. The pain made me lose my appetite and I lost a lot of weight. I have heard this referred to as "the divorce diet." I never felt like eating. I found myself in tears at the most inopportune moments. I felt sad, hurt, embarrassed, so much like a failure and humiliated by it all. Sometimes I wondered if I would ever feel like myself again. I also wondered how and why this had happened. I had been a good wife. I was certain of that. But it wasn't enough, which made the pain even worse.

I know many relationships fail and I am not writing this to make anyone feel sorry for me. It all ended up turning out just fine, but I want to be honest, share my experiences, and hopefully help others with similar stories.

The summer after we separated the stress just never left me. If I happened to wake up in the morning and feel like myself—it lasted for a split second, just long enough for reality to set in. All at once I'd remember what was going on and what had happened, and the stress would come flooding back. In addition to being a nervous wreck and not eating much, I stupidly started smoking again. Thankfully, I later kicked that habit.

We never had children. However, we did have our dogs (our "first babies," we called them), the custody of whom we shared. As much as I loved them, coordinating their schedules increased my stress levels. I remember one weekend when I had to go out of town for work. At the last minute Kevin told me he couldn't take the dogs. That left me scrambling to get a dog sitter to stay at my apartment while also keeping them out of the way of my roommate. The dogs needed to stay in familiar territory because one of them, Sassy, could become very anxious. When I tried boarding them with a wonderful lady I knew, Sassy refused to eat or drink. She got sick and I ended up in the emergency vet clinic with her while she was treated for dehydration. Situations like this led to more conversations with Kevin that evolved into difficult discussions that always left me feeling like I'd been punched in the gut.

It was a wrenching time for me. But, as promised by loved ones, time had a way of healing the pain. I didn't want to stay in that place forever. Sadly I had seen some people who did just that. Once they were hurt deeply, they never moved past it and talked about it constantly. I refused to have the victim mentality. I was not going to be defined by my divorce.

Thankfully, by God's grace, I was enabled to make some key decisions that allowed me to get on with my life. And the biggest decision I made was simply to go forward and look for the opportunities my new life offered me. The way I saw it, I could either stop and feel sorry for myself and allow the stress to consume me, or I could look ahead and go forward. I chose to do the latter. I chose to live and be happy. Even though I often woke up in the middle of the night filled with sadness and stress, I knew there was so much life out there to enjoy and I wasn't going to miss out. I gave myself permission to smile again, stay positive, and move on.

It hit me like a ton of bricks. I had always approached my career by saying "yes" to every opportunity. So why couldn't I do that in my personal life, too? I could. And, I did. My Jesus Year went from bad to great because I started saying yes to life and soaking up every opportunity. I was determined to take control. I realized I didn't need a man in my life to be happy—all I needed was God.

FOR AS LONG as I can remember, my mother has said, "In order to have a friend, you have to be a friend." She was always organizing parties and plans, and so as I tried to focus on myself, I took note and did the same. I planned group trips with my girlfriends and we were always on the go. We spent a lot of time in the Hamptons or Nantucket. We spent hours on end talking, laughing, and dancing our troubles away. Those weekends helped me heal and introduced me to a new world.

It felt like I was getting a second chance at life and I embraced it. I sat down and wrote out a bucket list of all the things I wanted to do but had never done. All my life I'd dreamed of going to France and Italy but I'd never gone beyond dreaming. Now was my time. I'd hardly taken any of my vacation days since I'd joined Fox News. I needed that time now. I scheduled a week off and started planning a trip with friends. One of them had an aunt in Italy and friends in France with whom we could stay. However, not long before we were supposed to leave the person called and said his aunt was sick and didn't feel like having company. That didn't stop us. I was at a dinner party and one of my friends said, "We have the week off. Let's go anyway. Let's go to France and just figure it out." So that's what we did. We booked last-minute flights and did the whole trip spontaneously. That felt good.

The trip was, in one word, amazing. I'd always loved art and my interest grew when my seventh-grade art teacher introduced me to the master painters. Mrs. Pollard was a beautiful lady and extremely talented. She taught advanced art at E .L. Wright Middle School. The class was not a requirement, which meant all of the students who signed up were very interested in the subject. She taught us about her four favorite artists, showed us slides of their most famous works, told us about their lives, and made them come to life for us. We focused on Claude Monet, Vincent van Gogh, Henri de Toulouse-Lautrec, and Pierre-Auguste Renoir. We didn't just study them. Mrs. Pollard had us make our own renditions of their works. That class had a permanent impact on me.

We visited the Musée d'Orsay in Paris, and I was standing in front of the actual Impressionist originals of all those slides I'd seen in my South Carolina classroom. Then we visited the Moulin Rouge, where Toulouse-Lautrec was inspired to paint the cancan girls. I could feel his presence there. He was an outcast and only felt loved and accepted at the Moulin Rouge. I was watching a show in the very room he once considered an oasis. The whole experience was magical and I knew I needed to thank Mrs. Pollard.

Sitting outside a café in Paris, I called my mom, told her the story, and she connected me to Mrs. Pollard, who was in an assisted living facility in South Carolina. I immediately called her from my table, the Seine River and Eiffel Tower behind me. I introduced myself and explained to her that I had been her student twenty years earlier and appreciated the difference she had made in my life. I went on to tell her about my adventures in Paris and how meaningful it was to see the artists' original pieces. I said, "Mrs. Pollard, you did this for me. You made Paris come to life. I've always wanted to come here because of you and now it's a reality and I'm living my dream."

That trip was a turning point for me. I realized how easy it was to travel, and the educational advantages you can gain from visiting other countries. I committed to traveling more often and was excited about sharing the world with my future children. I fell in love with Paris and understood Gertrude Stein's sentiment, "America is my country and Paris is my home town." Although America will always have most of my heart, I did leave a portion in Paris and continue to go back every chance I get. Recently I looked through a scrapbook I made from that first trip to Paris. On the last page I quoted Mark Twain, "Travel is fatal to prejudice, bigotry and narrow-mindedness." On my trips, I recognize cultural differences and am reminded that we are all God's children. We have different languages, lifestyles, traditions, and beliefs, but everyone is beautiful and God's creation. He is the greatest artist and creator I have ever studied.

I started to appreciate life in a different way and take it all in. I think in your twenties you feel invincible, but in your thirties you really start to live because you feel life passing by quickly. And, now that I'm a mother in my forties, I pray and beg for more time and a full life with my child.

AND SO MY thirties became all about living life before I settled down to start my family. I started traveling a lot. Not all of my trips were quite as elaborate as Paris. But I tried to make every experience special. Little by little, I could feel hope overcoming my past and new healing happening. I was still working hard, but playing hard. Often, I was about to leave for a weekend trip and Fox News would call. My boss would say, "A story just broke and we need you to fly out to cover it," or "The weekend anchor is out and we need you to fill in." When that happened I, of course, went to work. My job was most important and afforded me this great social life. But when the breaking news or the weekend shows were covered and done—I was on the first flight out ready to meet up with my friends. I was always seizing the moment and I preferred it that way.

I stayed active and it kept my mind busy. If I passed a restaurant and wanted to try something new, I did it. If I was invited on a trip at the last minute, I went. I was not only a "yes person" at work, I was a "yes person" at home. I only had to answer to God and that felt liberating.

At the same time, I was also given more responsibilities at work. I was being called on more often to cover stories, to travel, and to fill in on more shows. It was almost as if God was blessing me when I needed it most. Everything was improving. Many people at work asked me how I was so happy and content after losing my marriage. Even though my grief didn't immediately go away, instead I concentrated on the task in front of me—whether it was work or enjoying life. The fact that I was often reporting on difficult subjects only deepened my perspective.

Then, about nine months after the split I woke up one morning and felt like myself. I still had a deep-seated sadness over what had been lost and what might have been, but I didn't feel the stress and regret and emotional pain to the degree I once did. I'd survived, and the experience made me a much stronger person. Romans 5:3–5 promises, "Not only so, but we also glory in our sufferings, because we know that suffering produces perseverance; perseverance, character; and character, hope. And hope does not put us to shame, because God's love has been poured out into our hearts through the Holy Spirit, who has been given to us." God poured out His love on me when I went through my darkest days and His love gave me hope. God's hope never disappoints.

My Jesus Year was about making a choice. The direction of my life changed as a result. I decided to live for my many blessings and successes instead of focusing upon the stain of failure. I found the strength to focus on my own needs and decided to accomplish some of those goals. Nothing was going to hold me back and I was going to start to live my truth. I picked myself up and looked in the mirror and decided to like who I had become. Being in the pit, down-and-out, and feeling guilt or regret was awful. I didn't want to live there anymore. I asked God for forgiveness and to help me hold my head up high and follow Him on this new journey. I knew it would be good and I was ready to walk down that road. A year that started out so terribly continued to surprise me. That is why I hated to see it end. Jesus gave His life at the age of thirty-three and I felt like He gave me mine back that same year of my life. Once again, He saved me. I discovered His love and grace were more than enough to carry me through anything. More than that, I learned His love is truly unconditional. He loved me through the ups and downs and redeemed me when I needed His grace the most.

# 13

# *A Surprising New Chapter Opens*

> One thing I do: Forgetting what is behind and strain-
> ing toward what is ahead, I press on toward the goal
> to win the prize for which God has called me heaven-
> ward in Christ Jesus.
>
> —PHILIPPIANS 3:13–14

SLOWLY BUT SURELY I found I could breathe again in my personal life. Professionally, however, I was in a place of uncertainty. My contract was up for renewal at Fox News. In the years I
had been there I had become a regular guest anchor on the morning
news shows. My "Ainsley Across America" segment on Sean Hannity's show kept me very busy, and also seemed to be a favorite with
fans of the show. While I was still officially working overnights, the
network sent me everywhere covering stories as a reporter, not just
for overnights but for the network as a whole. I covered the after-
math of Hurricane Sandy and the Fort Hood shooting. I went out to
California to cover the Kate Steinle shooting and interviewed her
family. Later I went back to California for the anniversary of the
Ferrari car company and got to test-drive one of their sports cars.
All in all, I had every reason to believe I was in a very good place at
Fox News, but I had no way of knowing for sure.

The worry and uncertainty forced me to my knees in prayer to
God. Over and over again I laid my future in His hands. As my
contract situation dragged out to nearly a year, I realized I had no
control over my future. I might as well put it in God's hands since
it had been there all along! It wasn't like I did not have options if,

God forbid, my time at Fox News ended. I still had connections with people in the local markets where I had worked before moving to New York. Perhaps one of them might be willing to hire me. I had national network experience. I was quite certain I could get a job in a local market. If worse came to worst, I could even move back home to my parents' house in Columbia. I doubted I'd ever have to do anything like that, but I knew that their door was always open, which meant I'd never be destitute.

Wow. As I write this I realize how the mind plays tricks on you when you let worry and fear cloud your thinking.

As it turned out, all of my fears were for nothing. In the end, I signed a new three-year contract. What a blessing! Here I had all these fears running around my mind and God had it all under control the whole time. I knew He did. I did not doubt Him, but I am such a planner that it was hard for me to stand by and wait on Him when I could not see exactly what His plan was. I guess that makes me like the dad of the sick boy in Mark 9:24 who told Jesus, "I do believe; help me overcome my unbelief!"

Throughout my year of uncertainty I kept reminding myself of Jesus' words in the Sermon on the Mount (Matthew 5–7):

Therefore I tell you, do not worry about your life, what you will eat or drink; or about your body, what you will wear. Is not life more than food, and the body more than clothes? Look at the birds of the air; they do not sow or reap or store away in barns, and yet your heavenly Father feeds them. Are you not much more valuable than they? Can any one of you by worrying add a single hour to your life? And why do you worry about clothes? See how the flowers of the field grow. They do not labor or spin. Yet I tell you that not even Solomon in all his splendor was dressed like one of these. If that is how God clothes the grass of the field, which is here today and tomorrow is thrown into

the fire, will he not much more clothe you—you of little faith?
So do not worry, saying, "What shall we eat?" or "What shall
we drink?" or "What shall we wear?" For the pagans run after
all these things, and your heavenly Father knows that you need
them. But seek first his kingdom and his righteousness, and all
these things will be given to you as well. Therefore do not worry
about tomorrow, for tomorrow will worry about itself. Each day
has enough trouble of its own.

—MATTHEW 6:25–34

"Don't worry about tomorrow," I reminded myself over and over
again. It wasn't easy. As I said, my family had known that my contract was up for renewal. Whenever I talked to them they asked
about it. Finally I had to tell everyone to stop asking. I didn't have
any answers. I know everyone asked because they were concerned
about me. However, their questions made it harder for me to keep
my focus on God's promise. I knew I was much more valuable to
Him than birds or flowers. He is my Father. His love for me never
changes. He has a plan for me. I just had to patiently wait until that
plan unfolded.

When His plan did take shape, it was so much bigger and better than just a new contract. Not only did I get to keep doing the
job that I absolutely loved, but my responsibilities were about to
grow in a very exciting way. During the latter part of 2011 I heard
rumors that we were going to add a new program to our morning lineup, a program that would come on the air before *Fox &
Friends*. I wasn't exactly sure what the program was going to be,
but I knew I wanted to be a part of it. Throughout my career I'd
wanted to be the girl who said yes to every assignment. That is
still true today. However, when I heard the rumors about the new
program I didn't wait until my bosses came to me. I went to them
and told them yes even before they asked.

The program turned out to be a one-hour show early in the morning called *Fox & Friends First*. The plan was for it to come on at 5 A.M. and lead into *Fox & Friends* at six. When I heard the schedule I thought that it was perfect for me. When I was not on assignment covering a story somewhere in the world, I still worked overnights. I pitched the idea to my boss that I could continue working overnights, which would then lead right into the 5 A.M. show. And that's exactly what I did.

I will say I felt that I had grown so much as a person and a woman of faith during this time. As the bosses were rotating anchors and deciding who was not going to be assigned to the show I never really worried if I was going to get cut. I had learned to give my troubles to Him—knowing that He would make my path straight. I said, "God if you want me to have this job, please let me have it. But if you have other plans, please show me what they are."

Thankfully, His plans were for me to launch *Fox & Friends First* and be one of its two hosts. I got the job! I continued working overnights, at least for the next two years. Every night I went in at eight, did the overnight headlines, then slid into the anchor chair at *Fox & Friends First* from five until six in the morning. I usually went home at six and crashed for a few hours, as I had been up all night long and I could barely stay awake. It made for long days, but it was worth it.

MY LIFE BECAME a little more complicated one day when I received a message that said, "Hey, Ainsley. My name is Will Proctor. I live down in Florida. I know you don't know me but we have some mutual friends and I'd love to just talk to you and meet you." My first instinct was to ignore it. The last thing I wanted was to get involved with another man. I just wanted to be single for a while and figure out what Ainsley needed. I had started dating again, but only occasionally and nothing serious because I was still not quite ready.

But there was something about Will that led me to respond to his message. At first it was just a message. Then we started talking on the phone and everything seemed to flow. We had a lot in common. He was from Winter Park, Florida, but loved Manhattan (his grandparents were all from New York), and he had gone to college in South Carolina. He played college football at Clemson University. Even though Clemson is the University of South Carolina's biggest rival, him playing there meant he understood my home state. From the moment Will and I first talked, we hit it off. Our family backgrounds were very similar, as were our core values. At this point I still thought of it as nothing more than a potential friendship. After all, no matter how well we got along on the phone, Will lived in Florida and I lived in New York City. I wasn't looking for a serious relationship and I certainly wasn't looking for a long-distance one. However, the frequency of our phone calls increased until we talked nearly every night and I thought, *I have got to meet this guy.*

One day Will said, "I'm going to come up to New York, stay in a hotel for a couple of days, and take you on a date. I really want to meet you face-to-face." I couldn't say no.

The first date went by way too fast. When he asked me for another I immediately said yes. The second date turned into another and another and another. Before I knew it, we were in a long-distance relationship. Being in a long-distance relationship was more complicated than I ever expected. When we were together everything was great, but the distance between us made dating more difficult. At times we felt like two ships passing in the night because coordinating our busy schedules became increasingly difficult. For a long time I did not mind because I did not want to get serious, not yet at least.

The two of us dated for a couple of years before I finally felt like I was ready to get married again. I loved him, we had similar goals, he supported my career, and we both wanted children.

Eventually we started talking about marriage pretty frequently. I thought he was ready to pop the question. In fact, I thought I knew exactly when he was going to do it. He was supposed to come up to New York for the weekend. I took Thursday and Friday off so that we would have more time together. But when we started planning the big weekend, he said he couldn't come up. He claimed he was going to be in Augusta, Georgia, for a Clemson University golf tournament. That shook me. I thought he was coming up to propose and instead he goes off to play golf for his former college? Little did I know that at the time he was actually in Columbia, South Carolina, asking my father for my hand in marriage. My dad gave his blessing, and so did I.

When we first started planning our wedding, Will and I decided to have a small service at our church in New York. We'd first met in the city; we dated there, and it only seemed right that we get married where it all began. I'd already had the huge service and reception with my first wedding and I didn't think it was right to do that again. Will, however, had never been married. His parents came to us and asked that we have the service and reception in their hometown church in Florida. I thought it was a generous and sweet idea. So we said yes to their offer.

However, even though our plans for the wedding had grown, I still did not intend to wear a white wedding dress and walk down the aisle. To me, something just did not seem right about doing that, like it was a violation of proper wedding etiquette, according to my mother. Instead I planned on wearing a cream-colored cocktail dress. I might have stuck with this plan except one of his mother's friends came to me when we were in Florida visiting Will's parents at their beach condo, and told me she had gone through a divorce then married a second time.

"I heard that you aren't planning on wearing a wedding gown," she said.

"That is true," I said, before explaining all the reasons why I felt as I did.

Then she said something that made me see this question in an entirely different light.

"If you don't wear a wedding gown, you are depriving Will of the experience of having the doors of the church open and seeing his bride in her dress for the first time. If anyone judges you for that, it's okay. This is your day with Will."

She made perfect sense. I'd never looked at this question through Will's eyes, but I'm glad I did. In the end, I found the perfect dress and his reaction was exactly what I'd hoped it would be.

I actually wore a second dress during the wedding weekend. One obviously doesn't wear the actual wedding dress for the rehearsal, but I wanted to wear something special that night. A while earlier my mother had given me her wedding dress. Her mother, my Mimi, had sent it off to be preserved after my mother's wedding day, which meant no one had even touched it since then. The dress didn't work as a wedding dress for me, so I asked my mom if I could cut it off to knee length, have other alterations made, and wear it to the rehearsal and dinner. She gladly gave her consent.

A few days before the wedding we learned that my uncle, my dad's brother, my precious uncle, was dying. I decided to fly down to Columbia a few days before the wedding and spend time with him and his wife, my aunt Linda. They never had children, which meant they spoiled my siblings and me. We were and still are their "kids." My aunt couldn't come to the wedding. She obviously wanted to stay home with her husband, my uncle. I ended up driving down to Winter Park, where the wedding was to take place, with my immediate family from Columbia. On the way I said something to my mom, like, "Mom, your dress is so beautiful.

I love the lace. I love how the lace is at the shoulder and the lace on the arms is so beautiful. I had to expand it a little because your arms are so tiny."

My mother looked at me and said, "Ainsley, that's not my dress. My dress had an Empire waist and no lace."

"No, Mom. The dress I have has a boat neck with lace covering the arms." I went on to describe the dress a little further.

"The dress you're describing sounds like my sister's dress," my mom said.

My heart sank. I was so excited about surprising my mother in her dress and now she was telling me that someone had switched the boxes. I called my mom's sister, my aunt Lynn. I described the dress to her and asked her about it. She confirmed my worst fears. I had completely altered my aunt's wedding dress! I was so afraid she'd be upset. Instead she put me at ease and started laughing over the mix-up. "Ainsley, I'm so glad it's put to use. I think it is wonderful." She and my uncle had three boys, so I think she was genuinely happy I now had her dress. On the night of the rehearsal, when I walked out in the dress, my aunt started crying. We shared a wonderful moment, the first of many that weekend.

AFTER THE WEDDING, Will and I went to Palm Beach for a few days. We both had to go back to work and decided to wait a few months to take our big honeymoon in Europe. Six months later, in April, we flew to Paris. Will had never been to France, so we had a nice time eating at special restaurants, visiting all the museums, and seeing a few shows. We took a private tour of Moët & Chandon, which is one of the world's largest champagne producers, the maker of Dom Pérignon. At the end of our tour we bought a nice bottle of Dom Pérignon under one condition: we couldn't open it until the day our first child was born. We took a picture with the bottle and posted it on our social media sites—telling our mothers that they would enjoy that champagne with us on the very day they would hold their grandchild for the first time. The employees wrapped it in bubble wrap and I packed it tightly in our luggage. We then took the train to London and finished our honeymoon there.

A new chapter had begun. I knew God was, once again, making my wrongs completely right.

# 14

## *God Is Still Good*

Even though I walk through the darkest valley, I will
fear no evil, for you are with me.

—PSALM 23:4

I KNEW THAT when it was time for me to have a baby God would
plant that desire in my heart. Deep in my heart I always knew
I wanted to be a mom but the time never seemed to be right. It
was never right in my first marriage. At least I was never ready. I
wanted to be in a stable place financially and professionally before
I brought a baby into this world. I knew I could not maintain the
hectic schedule I had during my first several years at Fox News and
be a good mom at the same time. Maybe some moms out there can
pull it off, but I knew I couldn't work seven days a week and fly all
over the country covering stories and still give my children the love,
care, and attention they needed. I'm not saying it can't be done.
My mom was a working mom and she was incredible. To this day,
I don't know how she did it all. Now that I am a working mother,
whenever I struggle to juggle all my responsibilities, I just look to
my mother's example (and ask for her advice). However, for the first
dozen years of my career I did not yet have the desire to start a
family. The timing just was not right and I knew God would let me
know when it was.

And He did.

About three years after Will and I got married the desire for
children grew stronger and stronger inside of both of us. While
I still worked a lot of hours, my schedule had stabilized after I

became the anchor of *Fox & Friends First*. We finally were in a position to consider buying an apartment in New York, which was very important to me before starting a family. All of the details I wanted to take care of before bringing a child into this world seemed to be falling into place. On top of that, God just planted a desire within me to have a baby.

Of course, I approached having a baby in my usual, Ainsley Earhardt plan-out-every-detail way. I'd always heard how hard it was to get your kids into private school if they are born in the summer. I don't know the reasoning behind that. Perhaps summer children are the youngest in their classes and therefore have a harder time. Who knows? However, I made up my mind that if a child born in the summer has a hard time getting into the best schools we would just plan to have the baby in late fall or winter. That meant we'd get pregnant in February or March and there wouldn't be a problem. I had always considered myself to be very blessed and thanked God that things came fairly easily. So I naturally assumed conceiving a child would be no different.

It wasn't.

We gave it to God in March. No baby.

April rolled around. No baby.

And May. No baby.

Then June. No baby.

With each month that passed my desire for a baby grew stronger. Everywhere I went I saw expectant moms or new moms pushing their babies in strollers or little children playing. At first I thought, *How sweet. That will be me soon.* But as the months passed, seeing moms and their babies reminded me of what I did not have. There were those days when a tear streamed down my cheek as I walked down the sidewalk in Manhattan. In my heart of hearts I knew God would give us a baby, but it was going to be in His time. Let me tell you the truth: waiting for God's timing can be the hardest thing one ever does.

Will and I prayed and prayed for a child. We had our church family and our friends pray for us. Our families prayed for us. I had guests come on *Fox & Friends First* who, after the cameras stopped rolling, said something about how happy they were that I was open about my faith on television. Then they'd ask how they could pray for me. I always said the same thing: Please pray that I can have a baby. Some returned to the show months later and told me they were still praying. I was no longer worried about having a summer baby. I didn't care if the baby came in June, July, August, or September just as long as we had one!

Finally, after eight months, my prayers were answered. I knew I was pregnant and the test confirmed it. I was over the moon. Will wasn't with me at that moment and I wanted to find a very special way to tell him. Right after I got the test results I went over to Tiffany, the jewelry store, and purchased a small, sterling-silver baby spoon. That was meaningful to me because when I was a little girl my mother used silver spoons to feed my baby brother. She has a beautiful collection of silver and antiques, many of which she inherited from previous generations. When I asked her about the silver spoons in our kitchen drawer, she said she fed all three of us with them. A silver spoon seemed like a nice way to tell Will he was going to be a daddy. I asked the salesman to engrave our last name, Proctor, on the end of the spoon. The store then wrapped it up for me in their famous blue box, tied a white, satin bow around it, and I placed it in my pocketbook.

That night Will and I were supposed to go to a couples' Bible study at one of our friends' houses. This was the first meeting. I had done so many Bible studies in my life, but Will never had. Our friends didn't live far from us, so Will and I walked there. On our way I said, "I need to stop by our church to drop off some muffins for our church dinner [where we feed our homeless community]." I planned ahead and had even bought some muffins at the store earlier in the day. I just had this image of telling Will my news inside our church since this was an answer to so many prayers.

Will did not suspect a thing. He just said okay, and we wandered over to the church. We were already late, which made the moment more stressful than I had hoped. When we arrived at the church, the front doors were locked. No one was there. I acted surprised, which wasn't hard to do because I was. Since we could not go inside I turned to him on the front steps of the church and handed him the small, gift-wrapped box I'd hidden in my pocket. "What's this?" Will asked.

"Open it," I said.

He pulled out the spoon and looked at it, puzzled.

"It's a spoon," I said. "A baby spoon."

"What?" Will said, and then it hit him.

"Yes, we're having a baby!" I said. We hugged and celebrated the moment. As we walked down the streets of New York, toward our Bible study, the two of us talked about everything going through our minds. Will it be a boy or a girl? What will we name him? What will we name her? Can we afford private schools? We're going to need a bigger place! We talked about everything, we were just so excited. However, we had to gather ourselves and act like everything was normal when we arrived at our friends' house. We knew better than to tell anyone (other than family) until after we heard the baby's heartbeat and knew that everything was okay.

At eight weeks I went to the doctor and Will came with me. Eight weeks is a huge milestone. That's when you have your first ultrasound and get to hear your baby's heartbeat. Will held my hand as my doctor maneuvered the scope back and forth until it settled on just the right place. For the first time we could see our baby on the monitor and we heard the unmistakable *swish, swish, swish* of our child's heartbeat. I was absolutely giddy. Will had tears in his eyes. He pulled out his phone and we recorded the sound. I had never heard anything so precious in my life. We were really having a baby.

My doctor measured the baby and asked when I thought we'd conceived. She said the baby was measuring the size of a six-week-old not an eight-week-old. We didn't think anything of it and she didn't act surprised. As soon as we left her office we called every-one in the family. Will and I walked down First Avenue, talking to our parents on the phone and letting them hear their grandchild's heartbeat. The moment was one I never wanted to forget.

Before we left her office my doctor told us that she wanted to see us again in two weeks. She said something more about the baby's size. "Come back at ten weeks and we'll hear the heartbeat again." Perhaps we should have read more into her words, but we didn't. This was all brand-new to us. As far as we knew, every-thing was perfectly normal.

Our first hint that there might be a problem came during our ten-week visit. "I've had two other patients today that are going through what you're going through," she said, "and you know, it wasn't suc-cessful for them but I'm hoping we get good news for you."

I looked at Will and he looked at me. Neither of us knew what to think. My heart sank. "What do you mean you've had two other patients going through this? What are we going through?" I asked.

"Well, the size of your baby was small for where you should be. So let's have a look and let's see if we hear a heartbeat," she said. When she saw the shock in Will's and my faces she added, "I'm sure we're going to hear a heartbeat."

But we didn't.

Will held my hand as sadness and reality washed over both

of us. My doctor kept moving the scope back and forth. We could see our baby, but we didn't hear the sweet *swish, swish, swish* we'd heard two weeks earlier. We were silent and so was the ultrasound. I'd lost my precious baby. The official term is *miscarriage*. The word does not convey what you feel as you hear your doctor say the word to you. I put my hand on my stomach knowing that I had a baby inside of me that I could not protect and could not save. "I'm sorry," my doctor said.

I felt a peace come over me that had to be from God. "We prayed for a healthy baby and God answered our prayers." By that, I meant (for whatever reason) our baby was not going to be healthy here on earth, so my heavenly Father took my child to be in heaven with Him where she would be positively perfect. There this child is completely pure and healthy, with no pain or ailments, and in His presence forever. I didn't just hope this. I knew it. I know it still.

My doctor of nearly ten years was very compassionate as she explained the next steps. She scheduled an operation to remove my lifeless child. Even though my baby was now in the arms of my Jesus, a sense of despair washed over me knowing that I was going to be separated from my loving child until we meet someday in heaven. At the same time I wanted to put this behind me so that we could try again as soon as possible.

When we left the office, we made the very difficult calls home. I called my parents and Will called his. This child was both sets of parents' first grandchild. A few days later my dad sent me an e-mail telling me he'd been praying for me. He also said he'd been on his knees for days asking God why this had happened. I didn't realize until that moment how hard this must be on them too. They had been just as excited as I was about this child.

After the operation, the hospital conducted genetic testing

on my baby to try to understand why I had miscarried. We also wanted to know if this was a problem that might keep me from ever carrying a baby to term. The test revealed that by a fluke my baby had an extra chromosome. The chances that this might happen again were very slim. I was relieved. However, I had one more question. I asked the nurse who called to tell me the test results, "Can you tell me the sex of the baby?"

The nurse hesitated. "Are you sure you want to know?" she asked.

"Without a doubt," I said. I needed to know if I had a son or a daughter in heaven waiting for me.

"You were going to have a little girl," she said.

I had a dream a short time later. In it I was back at my dad's mother's house and my grandmother was lying on a bed on their back porch. The dream was so vivid, like I was actually there, even though my grandmother had passed away several years earlier. In my dream I was sobbing because I knew she was dying. I put my hand on top of her hands. I can still see her hands. She always had perfectly manicured nails. My sister then laid her hands on top of mine, then my mother came in and held our hands as well. All of us wept because we knew the end was near. Before I said good-bye I told my grandmother that I was going to have a baby. Even though she was so weak she perked up and was so excited. She didn't speak but when I woke up I felt as though my grandmother had reassured me: "I will take care of this little girl and she will be with me until we are all together again."

Some might say that this was just a dream, but I believe God sometimes gives us reassurances to carry us through difficult days. Looking back, I sometimes wonder why my baby girl had a defect that took her life so soon. But I also rest in the knowledge that God loves me just as He loves my baby girl. I don't know why He wanted her in heaven with Him, but I find great comfort in knowing that that is exactly where she is and I will go to her someday. My miscarriage—I missed carrying my baby—took me through the darkest valley, the valley of the shadow of death, and even there, God was with me.

## 15

# *Life Is Full of Surprises*

I have told you these things so that in me you may
have peace. In this world you will have trouble. But
take heart. I have overcome the world.

—JOHN 16:33

ABOUT A MONTH after losing my baby I had to have a second
surgery related to my miscarriage. My doctor worked me in
on the very morning I was going home for the Christmas break.
I didn't want to delay the operation because that would delay the
possibility of getting pregnant again. It took eight months to get
pregnant the first time. I hated to think how long it might take a
second time.

I know many women go through this and everyone has a
different experience. For me, I knew God was going to bless me
with a baby eventually. I just did. I was confident in that. I never
doubted God. The reason why is that I was exhausted. I was tired
of trying to do things my way and knew it was time to give God
the reins once and for all. I asked Him to bless me when He was
ready. At this point in my life I had surrendered all. I constantly
reminded myself that God saw the future and His timing was
perfect. There was a peace. I knew He was going to give me the
perfect child for me when He was ready and I couldn't wait to one
day be a mother.

Will and I immediately wanted to start trying to conceive again,
but by late January 2015 we decided to take a break. The stress and
disappointment were taking a toll. The two of us just needed to step

back, catch our breath, and work on other parts of our relationship for a while. For nearly a solid year we'd been so focused on having a baby. We needed to focus on us.

One night in early March, Will and I went out to eat at a Mexican restaurant with another anchor at Fox News and her husband. The four of us had a good time just talking and laughing. We told them we were taking a break from trying to have a baby. But when I woke up the next day I started counting days and realized I should probably take a pregnancy test. I called Will and asked him to pick one up on his way home from work. I casually took the test, waited and then —in shock—I called out, "Will, you need to come in here."

The two of us looked at the test and the word *pregnant* looked back at us. We were going to have a baby.

As excited as I was to see this, I was not able to relax or tell anyone until we knew our baby was healthy and growing inside of me. Thankfully, every doctor's appointment brought good news. At eight weeks I visited my OB-GYN. We heard our baby's heartbeat and got to see our child on the ultrasound. My doctor asked if we wanted to know the sex of the baby, but we told her we did not. We are traditionalists and wanted to be surprised on the day our child came into the world and announce the baby's sex in front of our family.

Even though all the news from my doctor was positive, I remained hesitant to tell my family. I didn't want to disappoint them later. So I kept our secret. One month turned into two. Two months turned into three. Each appointment brought positive news and I was ready to tell my parents. Mother's Day was a month away. It was never an easy day for my mom, as she missed her own mother terribly. So I decided to share the positive news on a day that was usually plagued with sadness. I made copies of two ultrasound pictures, bought a card that read "Happy Mother's

Day, Grandmother," and sent it off to South Carolina. I told my mom not to open it early.

On Mother's Day I made sure my phone was charged, the ringer was on, and the volume was up. The hours dragged on and my mom and dad never called. I finally called her at night and told her to open her gift. It seemed like eternity. She had to find her glasses and slowly proceeded to open the package. She said my dad was downstairs and continued to tell me about an event they had attended that night. I was so anxious and excited that I didn't hear anything she said. Finally she opened the card, read it out loud in a confused voice, and saw the ultrasound pictures. She said, "Are you having a baby?"

I said, "Yes, ma'am. You are going to be a grandmother."

She started screaming. I heard her call my father upstairs and together they started asking me question after question. "How far along are you? Is everything okay? Did you hear the heartbeat? What did the doctor say? Are you feeling okay? When are you due?" It was worth the wait to be able to assure them that our baby, their grandchild, would be arriving in November and he or she was healthy, according to our doctor. This pregnancy was the answer to a prayer.

I still waited to mention anything on air about my pregnancy, but viewers began to suspect when they saw me gaining weight. Eventually my body's changes made it impossible to keep my secret. One morning on *Fox & Friends First* I was wearing a blue dress and had my scripts in front of my stomach. When I made the announcement, I pulled the papers away and proudly revealed my new, little baby bump. I showed the ultrasound picture (one of the ones I sent to my mom in her Mother's Day card). I joked that I thought she was praying and my husband thought he was holding a football.

The response from viewers was overwhelming. I received so

many congratulatory messages and felt like our viewing audience was truly excited for me. I felt like we were going through the process together. I love those who choose to watch Fox News daily. They are my family. They keep me employed. They cheer me on and I want the best for them. Sharing the news with my Fox News family, colleagues and viewers, was just as exciting as sharing it with my biological family.

IT SEEMS THAT when God gives us blessings, He brings them in bunches. He did for me. While I had hoped that the blessings might come in the form of twins (Mom always wanted twins and so did I), it was not to be. However, every time I went to the doctor, I asked her to search for another heartbeat. I just knew God would give our family twins. But that was not His plan. God continued to bless me in other ways.

Years earlier, when I lived in San Antonio, an idea came to me during the middle of a church service. It sort of surprised me because my heart and mind were focused on the worship songs and the pastor's message, yet the idea popped into my head that I should write a children's book. Keep in mind, I had never before even considered this. Both my mother and my sister were early-childhood-development teachers. If anyone in the family was going to write a children's book I always assumed it would be one of them. Yet this idea kept growing inside of me until it felt like a calling, like it was something God wanted me to do. I responded and said, "*Okay, God, if You want me to do this then I will do it. I turn the whole thing over to You.*" My mind started turning over story ideas, most of which revolved around trees, but nothing ever really came of it. A short time later I received the call from Fox News, moved to New York, and got too busy to think about it.

However, the conviction that I needed to write a children's

book never went away. I continued praying about the idea and asking God for His direction. I knew God would prepare me for the perfect time. He eventually did.

I sat down, put pen to paper and wrote a children's book about something that was near and dear to my heart—one of my dogs. I had two Yorkies in Texas that moved with me to New York. Sassy was my first one. The experts would say she was perfect. She looked like a show dog—beautiful with a round, bear face, wide, gorgeous, brown eyes, and a precious, large personality. At a whopping four pounds, she was the quintessential alpha dog. Sassy did what Sassy wanted to do. She loved being around people and was not a happy camper when I left her alone.

I felt guilty leaving her at home during the day and decided she needed a friend. I called the breeder in South Carolina and he told me that Sassy's mother had had more puppies and he had a male Yorkie. Without hesitation I said, "I want him." My best friend picked him up and put him on a plane bound for Texas. When he arrived in San Antonio I was there to meet him at the airport and instantly fell in love. He looked nothing like Sassy, and to be frank, I wasn't even sure he was a Yorkie. I am still convinced he had a little Chihuahua in him. Regardless, he was mine and I fell in love instantly.

Saks only grew to be two pounds four ounces. He was never able to play or really keep up with Sassy. He was more like her puppy. She didn't need him, but he needed and relied on her. He was our little lover. He wanted to be with us constantly, slept on my chest or wrapped around my neck like a scarf every night, and worshiped Sassy. He had some health problems, which meant he was going to have a shorter life-span. Therefore, I held him close and cherished every moment.

After I moved to New York and walked Sassy and Saks on the streets people always stopped me. They would pet Sassy and then, always, make a comment about Saks's size. "Wow! He looks like a rat." "He is so tiny. Are you sure he is really a dog?" Sometimes I had to carry him (his legs looked like chicken bones and he walked/ran at a slant) and people would say, "Who's walking who?" I coddled him and loved him like a baby.

No one, other than our family, understood Saks. He didn't act or look like most dogs. He had so much to offer, but most didn't quite get him, and I wanted them to. So I thought it would be a good idea to write a children's book about him. I thought God could use Saks's story to help children understand that we are all worthy of love and have strengths. Therefore, I wrote a book about a little dog who gets bullied at the dog park and how he overcomes it.

Finally, the book was written. I had my story. What was I going to do with it? I first read it to my mom and my sister. Since, between them, they had nearly forty-five years of experience in the classroom, I thought they'd be a good test audience. Both of them loved it. Now, I am wise enough to know that a mom's opinion of her child's work is not always the most objective, so I took my book to my agent, who also loved it. She was with a large agency, but did not work in the world of publishing. Thankfully, her agency had a literary division and she connected me with one of the agents. When the literary agent said she also loved the story I thought I might be onto something.

The process of getting a book published is far more complicated than I ever imagined. My literary agent began setting up meetings with publishing houses. The first house with whom I met rejected the book. They had enough dog stories in their catalog, they said. We then went to Simon & Schuster. That first meeting could not have gone better. I went into a conference room with a banquet table full of women. We clicked right from the start. One asked me to read my story, which I did. I have to admit that I was a little nervous. Even though this was a children's book with animals for characters, there was a lot of myself in the story. I prayed while I was reading it that it would touch them, and their reaction put me completely at ease.

The conversation that followed surprised me. They said the book was cute and they liked the message, but then one of the women said, "We want to know more about you. We know you are an anchor at Fox News, and we watch you. Tell us your story." I told them about my life, beginning right where this book actually begins. I went back to my childhood and told them about waking up most morning to find notes of encouragement from my dad next to my cereal bowl. That sparked their interest. We talked about the notes and the lessons I learned. I quoted some of my favorites, like, "If you stay up with the owls, don't expect to soar with the eagles," and "I hope I'll never be afraid to fail." I also quoted his sayings about character, including "There are two things in this world that no one can take away from you, your character and your reputation." Since many of the notes had Bible verses in them, I shared a few of them as well.

When I finished talking about my dad, one of the ladies said something along the lines of "I think that is the book you need to write." As I've said over and over in this book, God's timing is always perfect. If I'd had this meeting with these ladies five years earlier, their suggestion would not have had the same impact. Talking about my dad and the lessons he tried to teach me as I was growing up made me think about all the lessons I hoped to pass on to the child that was growing inside me. While my dog book was cute and had great lessons, I realized the book I needed to write was not just for children in general, but for my own child in particular. I wanted to write a book for him or her that also honored my father.

The only thing left to do was write it, something I did not know too much about. More meetings followed with the ladies around the table at Simon & Schuster, who guided me through the process. Early on one said something along the lines of "Tell us what it's like to work at Fox News. How do you report on all the tragedy, the terrorist attacks and children being killed, and the murders and all the political fighting?"

I thought for a moment. "I anchored the other day on *The Five*"—a Fox News show in the afternoons—"and we had a discussion about the very things about which you are asking. On air, I shared a Scripture that came to my mind and helped me feel better about all the hardships we face. The verse is, 'In this world you will have trouble. But, take heart, I have overcome the world,' John 16:33." As soon as I shared this verse the ladies looked at one another and one said, "That's it. We have the title to your book." And that's how my first children's book, *Take Heart, My Child*, was born.

When I wrote it with help from Kathryn Cristaldi, I didn't know how the book would be received. Everyone told me children's books didn't sell as well as other books, something confirmed to me by the amount of the advance I received from the publisher. The book became something much more personal (in terms of revealing more of myself and my story) than my dog book. By that point in my life I had grown far more comfortable in my own skin. I was fine with readers discovering who I really was. That wasn't just true of the book. It was true in my regular job as well.

As I thought about writing that children's book and the message that I wanted to share, it became clear just how essential that verse "Take heart, I have overcome the world" had become to helping me through reporting on such tough news stories. Crucial as it was to my development as a journalist, the relationship between that passage and my job was not something that had sprung up overnight—it had come through reporting on some truly horrific stories. Perhaps the most difficult of these had come in in May

2013, when *Fox & Friends First* sent me to Cleveland to cover one of the most disturbing stories I've ever had to report. Between August 2002 and April 2004 three young women had disappeared in the same area on Lorain Avenue. The family of the first woman to disappear, twenty-one-year-old Michelle Knight, believed she ran away after losing custody of her son. The other two were only teenagers, sixteen-year-old Amanda Berry and fourteen-year-old Gina DeJesus, and were believed to have been kidnapped. Amanda and Gina were featured in a 2005 episode of *America's Most Wanted* and a 2009 episode of *The Oprah Winfrey Show*. Still, no one had a clue what had happened to the three of them. No one knew that their disappearances were connected until May 6, 2013, when Amanda Berry screamed for help through a crack in the front door of the home of former school-bus driver Ariel Castro. Two hero neighbors, Angel Cordero and Charles Ramsey, kicked the door open. At that moment Amanda ran across the street with her six-year-old daughter and called 911. Police arrived to find the three women who had been held prisoner and repeatedly abused by Castro for more than a decade.

I spent a week in Cleveland covering the story. Thankfully, this came a couple of years before I was pregnant. Otherwise I don't know how I could have handled it. As it was, the whole time I reported from Cleveland, all I could think about was the suffering these girls and their families went through. When the camera was off and I was by myself I thought about the anguish they had to go through every single night, wondering where their little girls might be, imagining the worst. When the details of the story came out I was horrified that something like this could happen in this great country of ours. I felt so very blessed to have the life that I enjoy, one that I should never, ever take for granted.

No matter how deeply this story affected me, I still had a job to do. And that job was to report the news and dig for more details.

One day, early in the week, I got a tip that the FBI was going to hold an as-yet-unannounced news conference, and went straight to the location of the conference and positioned myself where I had the best possibility of asking a question. You've seen news conferences on television. So many reporters squeeze into a small space, and if you are in the back or off to the side, you will not be called upon. After the FBI made a statement they opened up the floor for questions. I managed to be the second person at the mic. As all the national media cameras rolled I stepped up and said, "Ainsley Earhardt with Fox News Channel . . ." and then asked the second question of the news conference. That meant that no matter what network anyone happened to watch, they saw me and they heard my name. My bosses took notice.

The experience in Cleveland reveals one of the great paradoxes of my job. Here I was reporting on a story that still touches me today. My heart was broken for these girls and their families and drove me to my knees in prayer for them. At the same time I had to be a professional and report the story. The way I covered these families' nightmare turned out to be good for my career. My bosses noticed and commended me for it. That was not my goal. I just wanted to do the best I could possibly do, just as I do with every story I cover.

Ultimately though, I relied on my faith to get me through the darkness of that story. It's often impossible to understand why bad things happen to innocent, good people. And, to be honest, we never will understand. That is where faith comes into play. We believe in something we can't see, but we know it's there. God has a purpose and a plan. In this world we will have trouble, but I can take heart knowing He has overcome it all.

When I was a little girl, my sister and I were heartbroken when we watched a made-for-television movie about the kidnapping of a boy named Adam Walsh. It made an indelible impression on my life. I remember most of the scenes still to this day. Adam was shopping in the mall with his mother and disappeared. His mom was frantically looking for him and you hoped Adam was going to reappear. But he didn't. Adam was kidnapped and then murdered. I thought about the fear Adam must have felt. I couldn't shake it and clearly have never forgotten his story. To this day, when I report on kidnappings, I always think of Adam Walsh.

When I was in Cleveland reporting on these missing girls who were found, I was relieved to be telling a story with a positive ending. But I couldn't help but think of all they had gone through— the fear and grief. I was saddened that I had had such wonderful years at their age and these girls experienced ten years of pain. I hurt for them, just as I had when I watched the story of Adam Walsh. When I had to tell their stories on TV, I felt confident I was going to be able to report on the facts and show compassion. The story touched me and I think that emotion came across on air. The bosses had recognized that and praised me for my work.

After those broadcasts, more opportunities at Fox News opened up for me. In 2014, during the time Will and I were trying so hard to conceive a baby, Fox News created a new noon show called *Outnumbered.* It is still on today. The premise of the show was very simple. You take four female reporters or anchors, sit them on a big, curved sofa, and have them discuss the major news stories and hot-button topics. But they are not alone. There is a male guest who sits in the middle, who is usually an expert on whatever the big topic of the day is or he's a celebrity or one of the current anchors or contributors at Fox News. That's why the show is called *Outnumbered.* He is outnumbered by four smart, amazing women. The result is both entertaining and eye-opening.

After the debut of *Outnumbered,* I became a regular guest. As recently as a few years earlier I had been hesitant to fully be myself on the air and let our viewers see the real me. That changed on this show.

I loved being on *Outnumbered* even though it pushed me in terms of preparation. I could not just go on the show and rattle off an opinion without thinking it through. Being the planner that I am, I had to know every topic and study it thoroughly. Just like my days of preparing for a test in high school, I made pages and pages of notes, which I read and reread before going on the air. The show moves pretty fast, which meant I could not sit there and review my notes or read from them during the show. Unlike reporting from an anchor desk, there wasn't a teleprompter or anything else to read from. Instead I had to lean on my notes, my prep work, and speak from my heart.

The more appearances I made, the more comfortable I felt. And this was when I finally, after years of trying, was able to open up and begin to share my true self with the Fox News audience. The real turning point came during one episode of *Outnumbered,* which was aired while I was pregnant. Students at a college in California voted to remove the American flag from what they called an "inclusive" space on campus. The students claimed the flag endorsed American superiority and imperialism. This was exactly the kind of story for which the show was created. When the discussion came around to me I could hardly contain my emotions. The story infuriated me. Honestly, I think the flag represents America and every citizen. It represents the people who laid down their lives for our freedom: freedom of speech, freedom of religion, freedom to raise our children how we each see fit. I take the flag seriously. The red, white, and blue was draped over both of my grandfathers' caskets because they both fought in World War II. The flag unites all Americans, it doesn't divide us.

And that's what I said on air.

Our flag, I said, represents all of America, every creed, color, denomination, person or persons, every family, everyone in America. The red, white, and blue represents all of us, and here was some university telling kids they couldn't fly the flag because it might be offensive. Banning the flag—*that's* what should be offensive to every American who loves this country, I said. And, if you aren't proud of the flag, leave the country. Good luck finding a place better than the land of the brave, home of the free, I added.

The response to that show was overwhelming. I received so many e-mails and messages from people across the country telling me how proud they were of me for saying what I did. My bosses also noticed and commended me. I was thankful people responded like they did because the truth is, I couldn't help myself. I had to speak out. The experience made me ask myself, *Ainsley, what's taken so long? You need to start being yourself all the time. You've been too buttoned up.*

For years, I never let myself open up in that way because in the back of my mind I worried that some other network or station would not hire such an opinionated reporter if Fox News ever let me go. Fear and worry never produce anything positive. I let the fear of "what-ifs" keep me from fully taking advantage of the opportunity I now had. When Ailes hired me he told me to be myself and be genuine. He said the audience members are smart—they can spot a phony. I tried to follow his advice, but always to a point. But things were changing. I was open about my faith and it was accepted. I was open about my traditional views and it was accepted. The viewers and my bosses embraced it. Everything was coming together and I was more confident than ever. It was God's plan manifesting itself at just the right time. The best was yet to come.

# 16

## *Hayden DuBose Proctor*

I prayed for this child, and the Lord has granted me
what I asked of him.

—I SAMUEL 1:27

BY THE TIME my due date arrived our small apartment was
nearly bulging at the seams with baby gear. We were overwhelmed by the love and support from friends, family, and even
Fox News viewers who helped us get started. I loved seeing baby
toys, clothes, and supplies in my apartment. They made me all the
more eager to meet my child. My baby was coming soon and this
was another sign of God answering my prayers.

Our apartment wasn't the only thing running out of room. I
was too! When we first started talking about having a baby I said I
wanted a fall baby. Now that fall was here I was ready. One problem presented itself, however. About a month before my due date
we learned that the baby was breech. That is, instead of being head
down, our baby was feet-first. The news frightened me. My mother
had always told me how dangerous and painful it had been to deliver my older sister, who was also breech. (She should have had
a C-section, but her doctor made her deliver naturally.) The um-
bilical cord was wrapped around my sister's neck. She came out
unable to breathe.

I'd heard this story for years, so I was terrified when I heard
the word *breech*. While there is a process through which they can
get a baby to turn, my doctor and a few friends discouraged me
from undergoing it. It was not only painful, but if the cord became

wrapped around the baby's neck when it turned, the baby would lose oxygen and I'd have to have an emergency C-section. It was risky and I was not willing to put my child through it just so I could deliver naturally. I wanted to do whatever was best for my baby. That meant scheduling a C-section. I still held out hope that the baby might turn on its own. A friend told me that if you drink a Slurpee every night, the baby would turn. I thought it was worth a try. Every night, on his way home from work, Will stopped by the local 7-Eleven to pick up a Slurpee. I also did exercises to help encourage the baby to turn. Although I enjoyed the Slurpees, they didn't help.

There are many positives to having a C-section. I was able, for example, to schedule the actual day of my child's birth. My doctor gave me a choice between Friday, November 6, and Tuesday, November 10. I chose the Friday date to make it easier for my family to fly to New York. Also, it was a few days earlier than the tenth and I was ready to deliver. I wanted to meet my baby and have a decent night's sleep. Being pregnant was beginning to be a bit uncomfortable.

At the insistence of my amazing, understanding bosses at Fox News, I planned to take four months off after the birth. I felt guilty about being away for so long. In television, you feel a responsibility to your viewers. People are used to seeing you when they start their day. I felt like I needed to be there, but my bosses wouldn't hear of me coming back sooner. They told me this was time with my child that I would never get back. "Enjoy it," they said to me.

I hoped to do just that, but right before I was scheduled to give birth, the female anchor on *Fox & Friends* announced she was leaving the show to spend more time with her family. As the anchor of *Fox & Friends First*, I thought moving to the main show was a perfect fit. I already filled in for her whenever she took a day off. On top of that I regularly contributed to the show through newscasts and headlines. I knew I was most likely in the running for anchor position, but I wasn't immediately sure.

But then, for just a split second, a seed of doubt crept into my mind. *I'm out on maternity leave and I won't be at the forefront of their minds.* I had to snap out of that mind-set, and fast. I refused to let it spoil the time I was going to have with my baby. God had this, I reminded myself. He knows what is best for me and He will make it happen if it's His will. I just had to leave it in His hands. Besides, my worrying wasn't going to make the situation any better.

Before I left for maternity leave, I let my bosses know I was interested in the anchor position. I thanked them for their amazing support during my pregnancy and for allowing me to take four months off. Then I added something along the lines of "I would love to be the next female anchor on *Fox & Friends*. If you need me to come back early, I will do whatever it takes to make this work." Thankfully, I learned soon after that, I was one of the candidates under consideration and they did not need me to cut my maternity leave short.

ON NOVEMBER 6, 2015, I got up early and headed to New York-Presbyterian Hospital. When I moved to New York ten years earlier I knew this was where I wanted to have my baby someday. I even made sure that my doctor practiced at New York-Pres before I went to see her for the first time. The hospital has an unbelievable reputation and is equipped with a beautiful maternity ward. Also, if there is an emergency, God forbid, the doctors and nurses are some of the best in the world. The hospital juts out over the FDR Drive in Manhattan—my room actually looked out on the East River—and the views are quintessential New York, the city where all of my dreams had come true. It was the perfect place for my baby to enter this world.

We still did not know whether we were having a boy or a girl. If God gave us a son we planned on naming him William Bartlett Proctor Jr. after his father. If we had a girl we were pretty sure she was going to be Hayden DuBose Proctor. Hayden is my middle name and DuBose is a family name from my dad's side. My paternal grandfather's cousin was DuBose. I was told the DuBose family left France to escape religious persecution, and many of them settled in the South. The name fit perfectly, considering my faith is so important, and the DuBose family supposedly put their love for the Lord above all else and moved to America for religious freedom.

Both Will's parents and mine flew into New York a day or so before the delivery. My brother-in-law came too, but my siblings weren't able to make it. My sister had some work obligations, so she decided to come up a few weeks later for Thanksgiving. Meanwhile, Trent, my brother, and his wife, Darcy, planned on coming up but were in the middle of fertility treatments. The very day Hayden entered the world, Darcy's doctor said she needed to undergo the implantation of her future baby. The doctors fertilized an egg and they implanted it on November 6. Hayden's cousins (with only a 2 percent chance the embryo split and they ended up having identical twins) were given to their momma on the same day Hayden was born (about an hour after I delivered her). We laugh and say, "Mom and Dad, you got three grandchildren in one day."

Will and I went out to dinner at the Polo Club with all four of our parents and celebrated the last night of freedom. We called it "The Last Supper." We made plans and coordinated schedules for the next day. While I sort of regretted not having the whole Hollywood movie delivery experience (your water breaks and you rush to the hospital) the planner in me was happy we were able to map out the day. I was going to get up early, do my hair and makeup, check into the hospital, request a private room, walk into the pre-op room, and then the operating room, and meet my child. We told our parents to arrive at the time of my surgery and wait for Will in the waiting room. It was all set.

By this point in my life you'd think I'd have learned how pointless it is to make detailed plans. But I kept on planning and God kept on laughing. When Will and I arrived at the hospital, my doctor said to me, "We're running a little ahead of schedule. We can take you back now." So much for our best-laid plans. We called our parents and told them to get to the hospital right away. I threw my mother into a panic. "I just got out of the shower," she said.

"Well, hurry," I replied. I knew the surgery would begin and about ten or fifteen minutes later we would know if we were blessed with a boy or a girl. In my mind I had another version of the movie planned out. I would deliver the baby and Will would deliver the news, "It's a boy," or "It's a girl." That scene was not going to work if our parents were still getting ready or stuck in traffic trying to get to the hospital.

Shortly after we called our parents a nurse came in and asked me a few questions. I then changed into my gown and covered my hair up with the soft, net cap. Will also slipped scrubs on over his clothes, and put a cap on his head and the little booties over his shoes. The nurse returned and started my IV. Before long my doctor came in and said, "Okay. We're ready." I got up and walked with the doctor and Will through the recovery room. "This is where you will come after the baby is born," the doctor explained. When we reached the door of the operating room the doctor said, "Will, I need you to stay here until we get Ainsley all situated and we are ready to begin. Then the nurse will come get you for the birth." I followed the doctor into the operating room. This was it! We were going to meet our baby.

A nurse had me sit down on the operating table. She then opened the back of my gown and an anesthesiologist administered a spinal block. My doctor told me he was one of the hospital's best, which put me at ease. Thankfully, I felt the drugs nearly right away. My only fear had been that the anesthesia wouldn't work and I'd feel the incision. One of the nurses tapped on my legs then up to my abdomen and asked if I felt anything. All I felt was the sensation of pressure where I knew something was touching me. The doctor reassured me that the spinal tap was doing exactly what it was supposed to do. I did ask them to test it a few times.

Once I felt comfortable, Will was escorted into the room. He took his place next to me and held my hand as the nurses put a drape around my stomach area. Then my doctor said, "We're going to start now." Thankfully, I felt no pain as they made the first incision. Will gripped my hand. This was not the natural child-birth experience I'd always envisioned but at this point I did not care. All I wanted to do was hold my baby.

Perhaps ten, maybe fifteen minutes after the first incision the doctor lifted my baby out. "Well, Dad, do you want to come over and announce if it's a boy or a girl?" the doctor asked.

Will moved over to the little cart where our baby was and said, "It's a girl." His tone of voice was not what the doctor was expecting.

"Come on, Dad. You've got to be more excited," the doctor said.

"I am," Will replied. "I'm just nervous."

"It's okay. Everyone is all right," the doctor said.

Will then let himself get excited. Me, as soon as I heard him say, "It's a girl," I teared up. I just wanted to hold her. Before they handed her to us the nurses cleaned her and did a quick check to make sure everything was okay. It seemed like they were taking longer than they should. One of the nurses finally told us that they were trying to get her to cry. "She's not crying because she's tough," I said. Eventually Hayden let out a loud wail. It was the most beautiful sound I'd ever heard.

The next moment is one that I can hardly describe. Will picked up our little girl, snuggled her for just a moment, then put her face next to mine. I kissed her all over as my eyes welled with tears. I told her, "God has big plans for your life, Baby Girl, and I will do everything in my power to be the best mother. I have loved you and prepared for this moment for a long time. Welcome to this world." Hayden was perfect. For months we'd talked about who she was going to look like. I envisioned her as a combination of my husband and me. Instead my gorgeous little girl had the darkest hair and an olive complexion just like my father. I'd never seen anything as beautiful in my entire life. I just wanted to freeze the moment and hold on to it forever. I looked down at my baby girl, the little cap on her hair, and I felt love like I'd never felt before.

All my life I'd read how God loves us as His children. I finally understood what that meant. "Hello, precious one. Jesus loves you so much and so do your momma and daddy." I continuously whispered blessings into her ear. "God will bless you all the days of your life, sweet child. I get the privilege of helping you and watching all of your dreams come true. I will never leave you. It is a glorious honor to be your mother, my beautiful little girl. You are so smart and perfect for us. We have loved you for forever and want you to know what an answer to prayer you are. God delayed our plans for such a time as this." I still hold her at night and whisper these blessings into her ears.

When the nurses wheeled me into the recovery room, I vaguely remember joining a few other moms, but they were far enough away that we still had privacy. I had just delivered our baby and now it was time for Will to deliver the good news to our families, who patiently waited in the waiting room. A nurse videoed the moment as Will walked into the waiting room, looked around for a moment, then said, "It's a girl!" Our parents' reaction was exactly what you would expect. They cheered and hugged and cried and celebrated the first grandchild on either side. "What color hair does she have? Who does she look like?" my mom asked. Will just said, "She's beautiful."

Of course, everyone was anxious to meet her. The hospital had a rule that only two people could come back to the recovery room at a time. My husband was one, which meant only one of the grandmothers or grandfathers could accompany him. Will and I decided beforehand that my mom should be the first. And his mom had even graciously made that same suggestion. We begged the nurses beforehand to let both grandmothers go in together and one of them said, "I'll see what I can do." Thankfully, she was able to honor our request. They walked in, stood on the left side of my bed, and set eyes on the next generation. Hayden was in my arms facing her grandmothers. Will's mom just kept saying "Awwww" while my mom said over and over, "She's just so beautiful. She's just so beautiful." It was a moment that will forever be etched in my mind.

When they left, the nurse snuck back the two grandfathers. We have a photo of the most precious moment where Hayden reaches out and grabs hold of each of their index fingers. My dad looked at me and said, "How can anyone see this and not believe in God?"

After both sets of grandparents met their granddaughter, Will's brother came back and met his niece. And then, there was a surprise visitor. I was feeding my newborn child and heard a familiar voice. Linsay, one of my oldest and best friends, pulled back the white drapes sectioning off my little area and surprised me. She squealed with excitement and had her phone pointed at me. She was FaceTiming with Cindy, our other best friend, who wasn't able to come up. I had both of my dearest friends with me at the best time of my life. I felt so loved and in love. I was proud and happy we got to experience such a special moment together.

Finally, it was time for me to move into my room. A pediatric nurse took Hayden to weigh and measure her and do the initial newborn routine. Shortly after I arrived in my room they brought her back to me. A nurse asked if I wanted my baby with me in the room or to have her stay in the nursery. Of course I wanted her with us in the room. They wheeled in her little bassinet. Since we hadn't given the hospital our child's name in advance, the tag on the inside of the bassinet read simply *Proctor*, our last name. My husband and I spent the next few hours just holding her and studying her. We were blessed with a private room in the corner of the maternity ward, so our time with Hayden was undisturbed. That night we sat in the room with our families and, once and for all, made the executive decision to name her Hayden DuBose Proctor. We all agreed that it was beautiful and meaningful (having a family name was very important to me). Before we left the hospital we filled out the birth certificate, making the name official.

On our first day in the hospital, cards and flowers began filling our room. One card brought tears to my eyes. It came from the *Fox & Friends* and the *Fox & Friends First* staff and read, "We welcome the next American patriot into the Fox News family." That night, the hosts of *The Five*, which is a show on Fox News, announced to the world that Hayden was here and healthy. That evening, surrounded by friends and family, we decided to open the bottle of Dom Pérignon we had purchased in France and agreed to open the day our first child was born. We toasted to Hayden and God for blessing us with such a remarkable gift. Hayden was snuggled in my arms and I was drinking the champagne we bought years before knowing God would answer our prayer. He did and it was worth the wait. I was happy and my heart was full.

The next morning on *Fox & Friends Weekend* the anchors also announced Hayden's birth and showed a family photo of us in the hospital. Will had a bunch of pizzas delivered, which we gave to all the doctors and nurses who were working the late shift. We also had a candy basket we shared with the hospital staff. That was my sister's idea. We had a sign on the basket that read "Thank you for taking such good care of me and my mommy. Much Love, Baby Proctor." We were in good hands. All of the nurses and doctors were top-notch and treated us like kings and queens. I walked the halls that night, determined to start the recovery process immediately. After three nights, we were ready to take Hayden home.

ONCE WE WERE settled in our Upper East Side apartment, one of the producers from *Fox & Friends* asked if they could bring a camera crew over to the apartment to interview us and introduce Hayden to America. I was delighted. I felt like our Fox News viewers had been with me every step of the pregnancy and had supported me. I was ready to introduce them to Hayden.

The interview was scheduled to go live at seven thirty and the camera crew had to arrive at least an hour earlier to set up. If you have ever brought home a newborn baby you know that doing anything, ANYTHING, is more of a production than anyone can imagine. I got up at 3 A.M., which was actually an hour later than when I usually got up to do *Fox & Friends First*. I knew I had to get dressed and organized before Hayden woke up because once she was up, she had a way of taking all of my time. We experienced the same thing every new parent experiences: you wonder how someone so small can so dominate every part of your life! But I loved every minute of it. On the day of the interview I dressed her in a precious pink and white outfit, but when the crew came they handed me a *Fox and Friends* onesie. I gladly put her in this adorable piece that she got to wear because she was officially part of the Fox News family. My body still felt swollen from all the fluids that had been pumped into me for the C-section, so I put on black leggings and an oversized, light blue sweater. I thought the soft colors would look pretty in her nursery, which was gray and white—neutral colors since we didn't know if we were having a boy or girl.

The camera crew arrived; we set up and got ready for the countdown. I remember Steve Doocy asking my husband what the biggest surprise had been. Will said, "When we are changing her diaper and she isn't finished going to the bathroom. That's always a big surprise." We both laughed and so did the anchors.

When the interview ended and the camera crew left, I felt exhausted. After all, I'd just had major surgery. However, I also felt so very blessed by God. I'd prayed for a healthy baby, and He answered my prayer. He'd also given me a job at a place where I didn't feel like an employee. I felt like a family member. I felt like they were just as excited as I was.

I DIDN'T KNOW what to expect or how juggling my life as a wife and mother with my career was going to play out. But I also knew I didn't have to worry about it. God had given me so much. I knew He was going to show me how to honor Him in everything that I did. I'd always wanted my audience to see the light of Christ in me. Now my prayer was that my daughter would see it shine bright as well. More than anything, I want her to fall in love with Jesus and experience the wonder of being a child of God. Every night, when we say our prayers, my request is, "I pray you come to know the Lord at an early age."

# 17

# The Opportunity of a Lifetime

She gets up while it is still night; she provides food for
her family and portions for her female servants.

—PROVERBS 31:15

FOR THE FIRST three months of Hayden's life I never knew
what day it was. Most nights I slept in three-hour spurts.
I'd feed Hayden, play with her for a little while, then go to sleep
when she fell asleep. Three hours later she'd wake up hungry, so
I'd feed her and start the whole cycle again. I didn't worry about
my hair because Hayden didn't care about my hair. Forget putting
on any makeup. When you have a newborn baby, who has time
for makeup? Unless someone was coming over, I stayed in my pa-
jamas nearly all day. Whenever someone called and asked to stop
by, I always told them to come in the afternoon. I needed all day
to get ready. It wasn't that Hayden destroyed the house or we were
extra messy. The problem was I could only clean and get ready in
ten-minute spurts every hour or so. Some days I just didn't have
the energy to have company, so I started finally being honest: "I
really appreciate you wanting to come over and see Hayden. I
can't wait for you to meet her, but can we do it next week? I am
physically drained and need to take a break from having visitors
right now." I was just exhausted on most days, even though I was
enjoying every moment of being a new mom. More than that, this
uninterrupted time I had with my little girl was going by too fast.
Call me selfish, but some days I just didn't want to share it. I just
wanted to focus on her.

Having family visit was different. My mom stayed with us for a while and that was a huge help. I never leaned on my mother so much as when I became a mom myself. There were just so many things I did not know. You can read all the books that you can find, but they don't really prepare you for a crying baby who needs something but you have no idea what. In those moments you need your own mom—someone who has been down the road before you. I was so thankful she moved in for a few weeks. Will loved the home-cooked meals each night after work and was grateful my mom was with us during the days.

My favorite moments in those first few months came in the middle of the night. I got up with Hayden to feed her. Then she fell asleep in my arms. Rather than go back to bed, I often stayed on the sofa, holding my baby, sipping nonalcoholic beers (which are supposed to be helpful for breastfeeding) while munching on chips and watching movies or reality shows. I got caught up on a lot of pop culture I'd been too busy to notice. That's not why I stayed up, though. I loved just holding my baby as she slept.

Unfortunately, there were days when Hayden cried more than she slept. In the beginning we assumed she had colic. We tried all the remedies: my husband and I took turns walking the floor with her, rocking her, trying to comfort her. No matter what we tried, she kept crying. Our pediatrician told us that she was fine because her weight and all her other vitals checked off as normal. "Just let her cry it out," he told us. That's easy for a doctor to say. When you are a very tired, first-time parent pacing back and forth trying to get your baby to stop crying you find yourself pushed to the edge.

Hayden's crying went on for weeks. It was agonizing because I knew she was in pain and I couldn't find a remedy. I knew I had to figure something out because eventually I was going to have to go back to work. I could not leave my baby girl like this. Will and I read all the baby books. We followed our doctor's advice to the letter. He told us it would be best if I could nurse her and that's what I did. They told us that when she drank from a bottle we were supposed to give her a certain number of ounces, and we measured it out exactly as instructed. Because her weight was good I felt confident she was not crying due to hunger. I just had no idea what was making her cry.

I mentioned the problem to my best friend, Linsay. She'd also had a problem with her children crying uncontrollably. After she and her husband tried everything, she narrowed the cause down to her diet. She was able to determine that her baby could not eat the dairy and soy, which she was passing on to him through her breast milk. By this point I was desperate. Linsay had already planned on coming up from Florida to see Hayden. While she was visiting, we went shopping at a health food store. She showed me what I could and could not eat. That's not as easy as it sounds. Soy is in everything. With Linsay's help I found good alternatives. Unfortunately, the food I had to eat was not the healthiest. Most of the foods were fattening, the kind of food I hadn't eaten in a long time. But, if it would help Hayden, I was willing to suck it up and worry about losing the weight and eating healthy foods later. I just needed to stop her pain. I was willing to do whatever I needed to do for Hayden.

Linsay told me that it was going to take at least three weeks for us to see a difference. Slowly but surely Hayden's crying improved, although it took longer than I'd hoped. No dairy and no soy did the trick. By February, she was feeling a lot better.

AFTER HAYDEN WAS born, I did notice my prayers changed. I didn't care about myself nearly as much and spent hours each day with Hayden in my arms and prayers on my lips. I couldn't stop kissing her face and asking God to protect her life, place a hedge of protection around her always, bless her with friends, and always remind her how much she is loved. I will always pray over and over that God would give us a long life together and give me the tools to prepare her for the future. I pray that she would always know how much I love her and, other than Jesus, she is the greatest gift God ever gave me. I pray to be tough when I need to be, and soft when I should be. I ask Him for discernment.

THE FIRST TIME I ever left my baby for any length of time was right before Christmas, 2015. Hayden was around six weeks old. Fox News called and asked me to interview for the *Fox & Friends* anchor position. Perhaps I should have been nervous about leaving Hayden but I wasn't. Not only did I feel comfortable with our babysitter but I was interviewing for my dream job—something for which my little girl would be proud one day. If anything I was excited and felt like I was one step closer to another answer to prayer.

When I walked into Fox News and saw all my coworkers, the one thing I heard more than anything else was "What? You didn't bring the baby?" I smiled and said, "No, I didn't bring her today, but I will soon. I promise."

I walked into Roger Ailes's office and we talked briefly. He told me there was a list of women in the running for the job. I remember thinking, "I love them all and may God's will be done. Put the best person in the position."

The interview lasted about an hour. I knew he was interviewing other candidates but I did not feel anxious about whether or not I was going to get the job. Believe you me, I wanted it. However, if God had taught me anything by this point in my life, it was that my worrying could accomplish nothing. I'd been disappointed before, and while I did not want to be disappointed again,

I know that disappointment is just part of life. I had not gotten my "dream" job at Fox News before and the experience only made me stronger. If I did not get this position, I knew God still had great plans for my life. Rather than worry, I turned the whole process over to Him. "God, if this is your will, then make it happen." I went in for a couple more meetings in January. Each time I prayed and asked God to give me wisdom as I answered the questions. The bosses at Fox News knew me and they knew my work. All of the times I'd filled in as an anchor on *Fox & Friends* were essentially my audition tape. I felt I was ready. Like I've written so many times in this book, I left the rest up to God.

At the end of January Roger offered me the job. "Congratulations, Ainsley," he said. "The job is yours."

I had waited so long to hear these words, to get this opportunity. I felt like crying and shouting and jumping up and down. Instead I broke out in a huge smile and said, "Thank you so much, Roger. I would love to accept the job. Thank you."

Becoming an anchor on one of the network's flagship shows brought with it many perks that were especially helpful for me as a working mom. For one thing, I would have a predictable, solid schedule. That made it easy to plan and get child care. I had to be at work by 4 A.M., which meant I wouldn't have to get up until three or three fifteen. That was late for me. At the time, I was getting up at 2 or 2:15. The extra hour was helpful. Also, the consistent schedule would be great for raising a child. I was going to spend fewer days on the road and more time in the studio, in my office, and at home. In addition, Fox News provided me with an assistant (I never knew how badly I needed one until I got one), and a team of *Fox & Friends* producers and hair and makeup professionals.

The timing could not have been better. Once again, God knew what I needed and when I needed it. Uncertainty in my schedule and traveling all over the country were fine before I was a mom. But with a new baby I needed consistency and a set schedule. I also did not want to be out of town and away from her for a week at a time. My new hours seemed to be tailor-made for a working mom. Even though I go to work long before most people are out of bed, I can be home around eleven every morning. That means I get to be present for the best part of my daughter's day. Eventually, when she is in school, I'll be able to pick her up each day and attend all of her after-school activities. When I think of God's timing, giving me this schedule right when I needed it, I can't help but stand in awe of Him and give Him praise. Several years earlier I felt so down because I did not get the weekend job. Now I knew God had had something better in store for me all along. I just had to wait for His timing.

A couple of days after I got the call telling me I had the job, I woke up early and turned the television to Fox News. The show cut to a commercial. This was the moment my promotion felt both real and surreal. I watched as a promo announced that a new anchor was coming to *Fox & Friends:* me! My phone rang. It was my dad. "Are you watching? Your promo was just on television. This is really happening!"

"Yeah, Dad. Can you believe it?"

The promo ran again later in the day and then every day. Every time I saw it I said, "Thank you, God. You are really doing this. I am going to be one of the few national female morning anchors and the Fox News Channel happens to be the number one cable news network." In South Carolina and Texas, I'd always been so focused on what was next and working toward my goals that I never felt like I could just relax and take a breath. Now, for the first time in my adult life, I could. It felt wonderful.

I was excited about my new position and knew I had to work quickly to find childcare and get organized. I prayed and prayed about making the right choice. Because of my schedule, we needed someone to help us in the mornings. We started our search for a nanny and thought we found the perfect one, but it turned out that she had been diagnosed with cancer the year before and needed to start radiation treatment immediately. Her doctor cautioned her against being around a newborn baby given the type of radiation they were administering. That took us back to square one.

Thankfully, a friend at our church recommended someone. We interviewed her and instantly liked her. We actually had her come over to interact with Hayden in order to make sure it was the right fit. However, as January turned into February and the end of my maternity leave got closer, I started to feel guilty about leaving my baby girl. Between my husband and the nanny, I knew Hayden was going to be in good hands. But I couldn't help but feel I needed to be there to take care of her. I tried not to dwell on the guilt of not being at home full-time and reminded myself that many moms all over the world work and have successful children. My own mom was a schoolteacher for thirty-three years and had to leave us early every morning. All of us turned out fine and we learned to be more independent as a result. Plus, like my mother, I was going to have the afternoons with Hayden.

MY MOM WORKED to provide a better life for her family. When I go back to Proverbs 31, that is the very definition of the "wife of noble character" the writer praises. He describes her as one who "works with eager hands" (verse 13) and "gets up early while it is still night," to provide food for her entire household (verse 15). The wife of noble character is a businesswoman who buys a field and plants a vineyard (verse 16) and engages in profitable trade (verse 18). Vocations change over time. Proverbs 31 was written nearly three thousand years ago. I don't know about vineyards or engaging in profitable trade, but I know that when I get up and go to work every day, I do it to put food on my family's table. My parents taught me to save, and now I save as much as I can to secure a future for my daughter. The guilt I felt when I thought about going back to work, and the guilt I deal with on a regular basis just because I am a working mom, is nothing but a lie I choose not to believe. God gave me my family and He gave me my career. I want to be the woman worthy of praise who excels in both.

I remember talking to a coworker at my television station in Texas about being a working mom and she said she wanted her children to see her in a professional environment. She wanted to be a good example, teach them the value of hard work, and prepare them for those times she could not be there for them. She felt like that was a lesson all children needed to learn.

I asked my mother once, "As a schoolteacher, what is the most important thing parents can do to prepare their children for life?" She said, without hesitation, "Autonomy. Children need to stand on their own two feet and learn independence."

When I had to leave Hayden that first day, that advice went through my head. Was it easy? No. But I focused on the positives. I was excited to see my coworkers and talk to them about our experiences as mothers (I was now a member of their club). I could hold my head high knowing I was living my dream and that I was leaving one love (Hayden) for another love (my job). I had so many women whom I looked up to who had done it too, including my mom, and all of their children thrived and contributed to society in a mighty way. Plus, I knew Hayden would one day be proud of my accomplishments and it would make me a better person and mother.

To be honest, as much as we love, adore, and want to savor every moment with our children, staying at home with them is the hardest job. I applaud the women and men who do this. It is not easy. It is nonstop. Like many women, I choose to work, not because I want to be away from Hayden (not at all), but because I want to give her a great life full of opportunities. I like making my own living and it helps that I enjoy what I do. So if you have to work, hopefully you can also pick a profession you love. Although I crave "Hayden time" when I am on the job, I am happy at all moments of my life. At work, I get to do something for myself for a few hours and then I spend the rest of my day doing everything for my precious child.

Still, when I go to work, she is always on my mind. I am texting with my nanny during the commercial breaks and always watching videos from the day before with a big smile on my face. Hayden is my joy and reminds me of how sweet this life is. I will admit, there's no place like home. When I walk in the door and call out, "Where's my baby girl?" then hear her say, "Momma," and see her running toward me, that is, by far, the best part of my day.

# 18

# *Front-Row Seat to History*

And the Lord said to Samuel: "See, I am about to do something in Israel that will make the ears of everyone who hears about it tingle."

—I SAMUEL 3:11

I WATCHED A lot of news while I was on maternity leave, but the week before I returned to work, I didn't just watch. I studied every story like I was studying for a big test. In a way, I was. If I was going to talk about the news stories with my co-anchors, Steve Doocy and Brian Kilmeade, I had to be prepared. I felt the weight and responsibility to them, my bosses, and the viewers.

*Fox & Friends* welcomed me with open arms on that first day. When I walked onto the set and took my seat I felt like I'd reached the end of a very long journey. At the same time I knew this was just the beginning of a whole new adventure. Steve and Brian introduced me with a video of clips from my first ten years at Fox News, all set to music. Our producers and editors had put it together and I'll never forget how special I felt. Steve and Brian made me feel right at home, almost like I'd always been with them on the curvy couch. In a way, I had been. When the *Fox & Friends* female anchor or weekend anchor took the day off, I had usually been one of the first people Fox News called to fill in—for the last TEN years.

I had filled in so many times our viewers had seen me literally grow up and they knew me. They contributed to the woman I am today and the success with which I have been blessed. I will forever be grateful to them. I know they are out there pulling for me. I hope our viewers know how much I pull for them too. I want them to love their jobs. I want them to have happy marriages. I want blessings in their lives, good health, and lots of children and grandchildren. I want them to look at the generations behind them and say, "Our love created all of this." I want them to know the love of Christ and have hope for the future.

On that first day as the permanent anchor on *Fox & Friends*, I felt more at home than ever. Why? I felt like God put me in the position for a reason. I had confidence and assurance in that. I knew He was protecting me and watching over my daily experiences. Therefore, I had permission to be myself—trusting Him all the while. The Ainsley that found her inner voice on *Outnumbered* (when I talked about the flag) was the Ainsley I wanted to be on *Fox & Friends*. And, I allowed that Ainsley to come out again and not worry about the consequences. Since that February morning in 2016, I have been the real, genuine Ainsley and—like it or not—I never looked back. Living under the watch of my God is actually the most freeing, liberating move I have ever made. I can be myself and trust in Him to direct my path.

I don't believe in coincidences. I think everything happens for a reason. It was not a surprise that I joined the *Fox & Friends* family when I did. God gave me this job right in the middle of one of the most significant elections in the history of the United States. Regardless of how you feel about the results, everyone agrees that from start to finish it was one of the most surprising races ever. Not only did I get to report on it, attend many of the debates, and cover the Democratic and Republican conventions as one of the anchors on *Fox & Friends*, I also had the privilege of interviewing many of the key players, including the future president and first lady, the Trump children, and the future vice president and his family.

The first time I met Donald Trump I was walking down the hallway at Fox News near the hair and makeup rooms.

"Ainsley," he said to get my attention. "Hi, you are doing such a good job."

I did a bit of a double take to make sure he was talking to me. "Hi, Mr. Trump, thank you," I replied. I was baffled he knew my name. At the time I reported overnights, and he was a billionaire New York real estate developer, star of *The Apprentice,* and a regular on *Fox & Friends*. There was already talk of the possibility of Mr. Trump running for president, but I never imagined he would actually do it.

My first formal introduction to candidate Donald Trump came on August 16, 2016, at a town-hall meeting in Milwaukee hosted by Sean Hannity. I traveled to the city with a *Fox & Friends* producer and our crew (camera and audio guys) to give the Fox News viewers a behind-the-scenes look at the event and introduce them to the Trump supporters, many of whom had driven hours to hear him speak. As a childhood actress, I was very familiar with the small theater setting. That is the best way to describe the ambience of this town hall. Every seat was filled with the most enthusiastic crowd I'd ever seen, most of whom also identified themselves as Fox News viewers. One woman had driven up from Georgia. Another man I met had been to more than a dozen Trump events. I felt like the rookie in the crowd since this was my first town hall or rally (although I did go to the conventions, including the Republican National Convention in Cleveland where Mr. Trump gave his acceptance speech).

After interviewing the crowd at the town hall, I made my way downstairs, where all the town-hall guests were waiting. Sean Hannity had just arrived and I hoped to get a quick interview with Donald Trump. I knew it was now or never. Once it was taped, the future president would be escorted off the stage and taken to his car immediately. I had already requested an interview and was waiting to hear if it was truly going to happen. His handlers came in before he arrived. Security was sweeping the place and his staff was feverishly making sure everything was in order. We didn't see Mr. Trump arrive, but we could tell from the buzz in the room that he was there.

A few minutes later one of Sean Hannity's staff members came over and directed me toward another room.

"Ainsley, Mr. Trump would like to meet you," he said.

"All right. Let's go," I said.

I followed the staffer down a hall and into one of the dressing rooms. Secret Service agents and security were everywhere. They let me right in when I walked up to the door. The dressing room was like something out of the movies. There were mirrors covering all the walls and those large, round lightbulbs attached to the wall. Sean and Mr. Trump were talking and laughing. As soon as they saw me, Mr. Trump stood up, gave me a hug and said, "I am so happy to see you. I am so proud of you. Congratulations on the success of *Fox & Friends*. I understand your ratings are up thirty-three percent."

"Thank you, Mr. Trump," I said. I was blown away and a little embarrassed. Here he was, running for president of the UNITED STATES, and he's asking questions about *me*. He wanted to talk about my career and my success. In the midst of all his preparations for debates and speeches and rallies he had taken the time to check on the ratings of my show. Who does that!? I could see why he was so successful as a businessman. He genuinely cared about others. I remember meeting Bill Clinton at a party in New York and all the guests were saying the same thing about him: "He is very engaging and will make you feel like you are the only person in the room." I saw those same qualities in Mr. Trump and I knew instantly he had a good shot at winning the presidency even though the "experts" said he was going to lose in a land-slide.

Sean had to go back onstage, where he was scheduled to talk to the crowd before he conducted a question-and-answer session. Mr. Trump was going to join him in just a few minutes, but he said he was happy to do a quick interview with me before. His staffers told us how much time we had to talk to Mr. Trump. If memory serves, I think I had about seven minutes. I knew I needed to ask the tough, political questions first. I asked about the riots that broke out in Milwaukee the weekend before the town hall. A police officer shot a suspect who allegedly pointed a gun in his face. During the summer of 2016 many communities across the country were rocked by events very much like this. I was a little surprised by Mr. Trump's answer. He told me that the Secret Service recommended canceling this event, but he refused to do so. I also asked Mr. Trump about the grueling nature of the campaign, his upcoming debate with Hillary Clinton, and his first classified briefing as a candidate.

Those seven minutes flew by. A staffer held up his hand telling me time was up. I thanked Mr. Trump for the interview. As soon as we finished he walked out onstage and the rally got under way. The short interview he granted made the news the next day on *Fox & Friends*. It only took a few minutes and our viewers got a glimpse into his life and opinions. I went back to the green room and watched the town hall on a television monitor. This was one of many visits he made to Wisconsin during the campaign, a state the experts said he had no chance of winning. As it turned out he carried it on his way to his shocking win.

In October, about twenty days before the election, Mr. Trump's wife, Melania, invited me into her home at Trump Tower in New York to interview her. I was grateful for the opportunity and ex-cited about sitting down with our possible, future first lady. I also wanted to see the inside of their apartment sixty-five floors up. The camera crew had been there for hours setting up and preparing. They had a few cameras (one on Melania and one on me), which allowed the viewer to see me ask the questions and her immediate responses. More than one camera is assigned for the big interviews. The apartment was huge, with incredible views of Central Park and many of the iconic buildings in midtown.

When Melania walked in I was immediately impressed. She carried herself with such grace. Many people, especially in the media, had already prejudged her. I found her to be a very intelligent woman who speaks five languages. She showed me around the apartment and talked about the decorating, the incredible views of her "backyard" (Central Park), and the American Dream. She was an immigrant, became an American citizen, and lived on prime real estate. Most of the furniture was white and gold, the powder room was a rose gold and the molding and columns were gold too. I was curious to know if that was her doing or Mr. Trump's. She said it was her taste, too. She directed me over to a table full of framed, family photos, pointing out one from their wedding, one of Donald with Barron, one with her and her son, and then showed me her parents. I said, "That's your mom? You look so much alike."

"Many people say that," she replied. Her mother's hair was elegantly pulled back and she was beautiful.

When we sat down to start the interview, it was obvious Melania wanted to set the record straight. She told me the media reported information about her without consulting her to verify. I asked for an example and she referenced the *Daily Mail* newspaper and online site reporting allegations that she once worked as an escort. They retracted the claims after she sued for libel. Mrs. Trump accepted a settlement and an apology.

After setting the record straight about herself, Mrs. Trump

defended her husband against the sexual harassment allegations a group of women made three weeks before the election. She said the timing of the allegations was planned and the revelations carefully orchestrated. She said it looked, to her, like the opposition had put the women up to it. Rather than make these charges when they had allegedly happened, the women waited until just before the vote, and voiced their claims as a group to make them seem stronger. Mrs. Trump continued to stand by her man, saying the allegations were not true and should be handled in a court of law.

During the run-up to the election the *Washington Post* released a decade-old video of a lewd conversation Trump had with television host Billy Bush. The news broke two days before the second presidential debate. In that video you can overhear Mr. Trump making comments that shocked the nation. When I heard them, my heart immediately went out to his wife. I asked Mrs. Trump about the incident and she said the comments were offensive. However, she said she had accepted her husband's apology and they had decided to move on as a couple.

I then asked her about being on the campaign trail. Like the spouses of many political figures, finding herself in the middle of a presidential campaign was never something she thought would happen to her. I mentioned how many people wanted to see more of her. Her answer resonated with me. She told me that she had a son to raise and that he was her first priority. "My husband is running for president," she added, "not me. My top priority is to be a mother." As a new mom, I thought I would do the same thing.

Throughout the interview I was impressed by her strength. When one of the tabloids wrote a horrible, false story about her, she sued them. And won! Clearly this was a woman one should never underestimate.

My first interview with Ivanka Trump, which I'd tried to land for some time, occurred the day before she gave a speech at the Republican National Convention. Over the course of the campaign Ivanka emerged as one of her father's most trusted advisers. I explored that relationship by asking her what she says to her dad when he does something she disagrees with. She told me that she is very candid in expressing her opinions with her father. However, she always does this privately. He listens to her, she told me, weighs what she says, then draws his own conclusions. We went on to talk about what it was like to grow up in the home of a billionaire. She described how her father's example taught her the value of hard work. She said he was a great father and was there when she needed him. In middle school, she would sneak into the janitor's closet every day and make a collect phone call to him. She said he always took her calls no matter how busy he was.

In addition to the Trump family I also landed one of the first interviews with Mike Pence after he was named Trump's running mate. I flew to Indianapolis, where I met then-Governor Pence, his wife, Karen, and one of their three children, daughter Charlotte, at the Indiana governor's residence. In Indiana the governor's home is not called a mansion, as it is in many states, and this seemed like the perfect fit for the Pence family. They told me a wonderful story about the night they received the call telling them that Republican nominee Donald Trump was coming to the governor's residence for a breakfast meeting. The Pences do not have an extensive staff. They called a local restaurant to arrange for food for the next day. Then Mr. and Mrs. Pence got their home ready. The two of them were outside in Mrs. Pence's flower garden at 1 A.M. cutting the flowers that adorned the table when Mr. Trump arrived. That told me so much about the future vice president and his wife. They truly are a family with whom what you see is exactly what you get.

One of my favorite moments during the interview came when I

asked the Pences what they did when Mr. Trump called and asked him to be his vice-president. Karen answered.

She said, "Honestly, Ainsley, we prayed for the other people who were in the running."

I felt such humility in that response. Later Charlotte showed me a plaque she'd made for her dad that she called her "He Said to Me" plaque. It said, "Do the right thing, then go home for dinner." She went on to say how her dad always told her words of wisdom throughout her childhood. It reminded me so much of my father and gave me a newfound respect for Governor Mike Pence.

Eric Trump, the son of President Trump, later told me a story about how Vice President Pence became his father's running mate. Eric said he, his dad, and some of the campaign staff flew to Indianapolis for a campaign rally with Governor Pence. The Governor introduced Donald Trump, they had the rally, and then Trump was supposed to leave, but there was a small piece of debris on the runway which punctured the wheel of the plane. That forced them to spend the night in Indianapolis. As they left the rally, they decided to get dinner back at the hotel. Donald Trump, Governor Pence, Karen Pence, and Eric Trump sat in a small back room at the hotel's steak house and had an amazing conversation. Eric said, "It was fun to see that bond materialize. The conversation went so well, my dad had everyone else fly in the next morning to meet at the Governor's residence for breakfast. The Governor and his wife picked the flowers from their garden, which were used as centerpieces. They called a local breakfast restaurant to deliver the food and then asked if they could start the meal in prayer."

Eric says they sat there as two families around the table and history was made, "You could very easily argue that the small piece of metal on a runway had a large part in shaping the vice presidency of the United States and the election as a whole. All I know is we each flew about six hundred other legs during that campaign and we never encountered any other metal shards that left us stranded—only that night."

Of all the history makers in the 2016 election that I interviewed, there was one notable omission: Hillary Clinton. It wasn't for lack of trying on my part. I reached out to the Clinton campaign on a regular basis. Over time I got to know some of the people on her staff. A few came on *Fox & Friends* for interviews, but Mrs. Clinton never did. I think she accepted one interview on Fox News during the entire campaign, and that's going all the way back to the Democratic primary season. I assumed she didn't think she needed to speak to our audience. From the day she announced her candidacy everyone knew she was going to be the Democratic nominee. The primaries felt like little more than a formality. Even with that, she ran into some rough patches and lost some of the primaries to Bernie Sanders.

Of course, in the end Mrs. Clinton did win the nomination and everyone in the mainstream media assumed she'd easily win the presidency. I often wonder what might have happened if she had come on *Fox & Friends* and opened herself up to our questions. Surveys show that a large number of political independents watch Fox News. To me, *Fox & Friends* was the perfect show for her to visit. We had a lot of viewers who were undecided, and the 2016 election was decided by independents. I can't help but think she missed out on a huge opportunity. If I were in her shoes and I had the opportunity to make my case I would want to make it to the widest possible audience—whether they agreed or disagreed with me. Perhaps they would see a side of me they'd never seen before and I would get more votes. It seemed like a no-brainer to me. But not to Mrs. Clinton. She never came on our show as a presidential candidate. I believe that told our audience she wasn't interested in their votes. I will always believe that was a mistake on her part.

On election night, November 8, 2016, I stayed up late waiting to see who won just like the rest of America. I had to get up at 3 A.M. to get ready for work, but I had to know in real time. I watched Megyn Kelly, Chris Wallace, and Bret Baier on Fox News as one state after another came in for Mr. Trump. When they called Pennsylvania for Trump, the election was over. Results were still coming in from the West Coast, but it didn't matter. Pennsylvania pushed him over the top in the electoral college. Some in the mainstream media cried foul when Hillary Clinton ended up winning the popular vote, but that rings very hollow for me. Since the Constitution was ratified in 1789, the president has always been elected through the Electoral College. Donald Trump crafted his strategy around winning the key states to take the presidency. By doing so he ignored states like California, where he knew he was going to lose. Instead he spent a great deal of time in Michigan, Wisconsin, and Pennsylvania, states the Democrats assumed they'd win, so they ignored them. In the end, those states gave us our next president.

I watched the election results, and then talked about them the next day on *Fox & Friends*. Those moments were surreal. I didn't just get to cover history as a reporter—I found myself in the middle of the story as it unfolded. The year was an experience I will never forget.

The day before the inauguration I landed the last interview with President-elect Trump before he became the forty-fifth president of the United States of America. He was relaxed and rested. All of his hard work, time, and financial contributions had paid off. I asked him, "After you are inaugurated, what is the first thing you will do?"

"Go to work," he said.

He said he had already written and practiced his inauguration address and the first line was a thank-you to the past presidents, including President Obama and First Lady Michelle. He said they were very gracious and helped him make the transition smooth.

The president-elect said, "No matter how many times you step foot into the White House it is always incredible."

Mr. Trump also said it is a tradition for the president's entire family to sleep in the White House the night of the inauguration and they were planning on doing just that. That was the night his son Eric told the entire family he and his wife, Lara, were having a baby.

I have since been to the White House for different occasions and interviews. The first time I went to 1600 Pennsylvania Avenue to interview President Trump, I was escorted to the Oval Office through the White House hallways, which are adorned with oil paintings of our past presidents and first ladies. I saw Jackie Kennedy's face and realized my feet were walking where she once walked. I was mesmerized by every detail, tried soaking it all in. I kept thinking, *If these walls could talk. . . What joys, what sorrows, and what news had been shared in this home? What decisions were made here? What secrets were harbored?*"

I was later invited to attend a White House Historical Society celebration of Jackie Kennedy Onassis. As part of the celebration they showed a video of her in the White House, walking down one of the halls I'd just walked down. That's when it hit me again: I have absolutely the greatest job on earth. God has given me a front-row seat to history, and an opportunity to share my experiences with our devoted, loyal viewers at home.

I hope I never get used to this.

# 19

## *Moved, Stretched, Changed*

The life of mortals is like grass, they flourish like a
flower of the field;
The wind blows over it and it is gone, and its place
remembers it no more.
But from everlasting to everlasting the Lord's love
is with those who fear him.

—PSALM 103:15–17

A WEEK AFTER the election and Hayden's first birthday, she
made a live, in-studio appearance on *Fox & Friends* along
with my dad and husband. They came on the show for the launch
of my first children's book, *Take Heart, My Child*, which I wrote
when I was pregnant. In fact, I read the proofs of the book for the
very first time in our apartment while sitting in the gray rocking
chair in Hayden's nursery. At the time we didn't know if we were
having a boy or a girl. As I read the book out loud, thinking about
the child I would soon hold in my arms, my mind went back to my
dad leaving his notes next to my cereal bowl and the prayers God
had answered by making me a mother. I wept. The book itself was
not released for another year, which is pretty normal in the world
of publishing, but I knew on that day in the nursery that I wanted
my father and daughter to be a part of the event.

I received my copies a few weeks before it was available in
stores. The finished product was more beautiful than I could have
ever imagined. Artist Jaime Kim did a marvelous job with the watercolor illustrations. She wonderfully captured the essence of my

favorite South Carolina beaches and the trees of my childhood, and even included butterflies on most of the pages. When I noticed the butterflies, I thought of my maternal grandfather, who helped me with my insect project in second grade and suggested I choose the monarch butterfly to research. He told me he saw them on the golf course (he was an avid, scratch golfer) and asked our family to always think of him when we saw one. In fact, we have seen them flying around at each of our weddings (four of the grandchildren are married), and even though he is gone, they remind us that he's still with us.

I also loved the dedication page and the back cover. I dedicated the book to Hayden. My hope is that its words stick with her the way my father's words have stuck with me and guided me throughout my life. I wanted the world to know the role my parents played in inspiring the book. The back cover tells the story behind the story.

I shared with my readers the memory of my mother's hard work as a schoolteacher who had to go to work early, and how, as a result, my dad was responsible for breakfast. I wrote about the notes with poems, Scriptures, or sayings scribbled on a piece a paper that he left next to our cereal bowls. In a way, the story behind the story of *Take Heart, My Child* provided the inspiration for the book you are now reading. My books would not have been written without my parents.

I had high hopes for *Take Heart, My Child*. Every author does. The publisher was quite enthusiastic but also realistic. They know how hard it can be to publish children's books. Still, I had a feeling that God had bigger plans for this book. I couldn't wait for it to come out. A year later, when it finally hit the bookstores I was ecstatic.

The publishers might not have had great expectations, but the *Fox & Friends* audience proved them wrong. The book immediately shot to number one on the *New York Times* best-seller list. We sold out the first edition in a few days. I started receiving messages from viewers telling me they wanted to buy it as a Christmas present but couldn't find it. The stores couldn't keep it in stock. We hadn't printed enough copies because we were not anticipating such a success. In addition, I wanted the book printed in America (even though this was more expensive, so we had to cut costs elsewhere) and the publishers said they could have produced reprints faster had we originally printed in China. Thankfully we found another printer, who helped us whip out additional high-quality books quickly. That was a miracle and only happened because the CEO of that printing company watched *Fox & Friends* and knew we needed additional books. What a blessing! We ended up doing multiple reprints. In fact, my first children's book sold so well so fast that the publishers immediately asked for a second book. *Through Your Eyes* was released in November 2017 and also debuted at number one on the *New York Times* list, and stayed there for a few weeks and then hit the list again weeks later at Christmas.

At Fox News, we always talk about our audience being our friends. That's why *Fox & Friends* was given its name. Our viewers don't just watch us read the news—we interact, we have a relationship with each other. The publication of both of my children's books revealed how special that relationship really is. I had the privilege of traveling around the country for book signings and other promotional events. I was blown away by those who stood in line for hours to have me sign their copy of *Take Heart, My Child*. We hugged and took selfies together. Their response reminded me once again what a privilege it is to work where I do. I cannot imagine that any other network has such a special relationship with its audience.

I think part of what makes those relationships is the freedom we're given to react to the stories we report. When I was a little girl I used to watch the news with my mother. Many times I asked her about the anchors: "How can she report that without crying?" I still feel that today. After working in broadcast journalism for so many years I have become adept at delivering bad news to good people. Some days I feel a little like a doctor must feel when he has to deliver terrible news to a cancer patient. Most days I am able to present the news professionally, holding my emotions in check. However, that does not mean I am unmoved by the stories.

When the news broke about the Syrian government's use of chemical weapons against families, I was horrified. I thought about that story when I left work that day. During my quiet times with God I prayed for the people who suffered so much and thanked Him for protecting Americans from that type of a leader or regime. When terrible things happen to little children I not only pray for these families, I also cover my own child with a prayer that her future will be safe from such atrocities. I think most moms in America probably do the same for their children.

My time with God does give me peace when reporting on stories that are just plain frightening. As I write this, the news is still filled with stories about the tensions between the world and North Korea. Their dictator oppresses his people, starves them, and boasts of having the ability to drop nuclear weapons on the United States. Instead of letting panic fill my heart, I continually go back to the fact that God is still on His throne and history is in His hands. My heart aches for the people in North Korea who are basically held captive by Kim Jong-un with no chance of escape short of death. I pray someday they are set free.

I do not just report the news. The news touches me. Few stories have touched me like that of Sergeant Joel Tavera, a nineteen-year-old volunteer firefighter from Queens who enlisted in the army. Serving in the military runs deep in Joel's family. His father was a marine. In the fall of 2007 Joel was deployed to Iraq. The next March the humvee in which he was riding was attacked. Five rockets hit the vehicle, killing three brave men. The first soldiers on the scene thought Joel was dead too, but he survived. However, the attack robbed him of his sight while also leaving him burned over more than 60 percent of his body. Sergeant Tavera also lost his right leg and four fingers on his left hand, and suffered a traumatic brain injury. For his service he received the Bronze Star and the Purple Heart.

I met Joel when I flew down to his new home in Tampa, Florida. An organization called Building Homes for Heroes had just built a new home for him, a home they gave him mortgage-free. The amazing organization had the builders outfit the house to serve Joel's needs—larger showers, larger doorframes, and even a pool with a special type of water for burn patients. A man named Andy Pujol founded the company in 2006 in order to make a significant difference in the lives of wounded American service members and their families. They either build or modify homes not only to give the wounded hero a home without the financial burden of a mortgage, but also to help the vet live a more independent and productive life. After Andy lost friends in 9/11, he quit his Wall Street job and started the company. He has since helped thousands of our veterans.

Sergeant Joel Tavera had just moved into his home when I met him. His parents left New York and moved down to Tampa to be with him as he endured countless surgeries. His mom and dad described seeing their son in the hospital after his accident. They told me that they left everything to take care of him and also showed me pictures of him growing up. I have reported stories about the sacrifices our troops make to secure our freedom, but Joel and his family paid such a high price. Yet, rather than sink down into bitterness and anger, Sergeant Tavera adopted an attitude that inspired me. He was so happy and loving. I couldn't help but think of all that he had lost, and all he might never experience. I wondered if he would ever get married and have children or if he'd ever have a normal life. Despite countless surgeries, he never complained. I can honestly say I have not been the same since I met him. He made me want to be a better person, to live my life in a better way, to make a difference. Joel and I kept in touch and I have gotten a little involved with Building Homes for Heroes. How could I not? By the way, once again our viewers proved to be amazing. After we talked about the organization on Sean Hannity's show one night, the organization raised enough money to build many more homes for severely wounded veterans.

I was also touched by another organization that helps our troops and their families, Folds of Honor, which was founded by Major Dan Rooney. Dan is a fighter pilot who served three tours of duty in Iraq. He's also a PGA golf professional and overall just an amazing man and American hero. On the flight home from his second tour of duty, something happened that changed Dan's life. As he walked back to his seat in coach he passed a young soldier in full uniform sitting in first class. When the plane landed the pilot asked all the passengers to stay in their seats for a few minutes. "We have unfortunately a hero that died fighting for our country. His casket is going to be taken off the plane and rolled over the tarmac to his family. Please, out of respect, we ask you to remain in your seats until we are able to do this," the pilot said.

Dan watched out the window as Corporal Brad Bucklin's flag-draped casket was taken from the plane. Walking alongside it was the soldier Dan had passed in first class, who turned out to be Corporal Brock Bucklin, the twin brother of the deceased. Waiting on the far side of the tarmac stood a little boy. Dan later learned this was Brad's four-year-old son. As Dan watched the little boy standing next to his father's casket, his heart broke. The father of five daughters, Dan saw this unfold through the eyes of a dad. *Who is going to teach him to play ball? Who is going to take him fishing? Who is going to do all the things only a dad can do? Who is going to teach him about life?* Dan wondered. Right then and there he made up his mind that he had to do something. That is how Folds of Honor was born. At the time of this writing Major Rooney's organization has raised over $100 million to provide scholarships to the family members of soldiers killed or disabled in combat. He called it Folds of Honor because there are thirteen folds in the flag they give to family members of a deceased soldier.

The response to Major Rooney's appearance on our show has been amazing. The work of Folds of Honor made such an impact on me that I wanted to be a part of their work. A portion of the sales of my children's books goes directly to the organization. Major Rooney's organization earned a Goldstar Platinum seal of approval which means when you give to them, you can give with confidence. Ninety percent of the money donated goes back to the children.

I had the pleasure of presenting Major Rooney with a $50,000 check, thanks to everyone who purchased my children's books. My dad, who served in the Army Reserves for twenty years, put himself through college. He worked many jobs to pay off his education and his goal was to put all three of his kids through school. He did that. The day I presented the check to Folds of Honor, I told my dad, "Well, Dad, now you are sending ten more children to college."

Many other stories have touched me through the years. Of course, 9/11 did. It's still emotional for me and all of America. We will never forget those images or the heartache.

I was also affected by the excruciating death of little Jovonie Ochoa in San Antonio, Texas, when I worked there. Jovonie was only four years old when he was found dead. His hands and mouth had been duct-taped by his family and he was skin and bones. He was four years old and only weighed sixteen pounds. That is the size of a six-month-old. His family starved him and abused him. Despite his pleas for food no one helped him. I saw the pictures of his bony body when he took his last breath and wondered how in the world anyone could do that to a child. I wondered why I couldn't rescue him and then wondered how many other children were out there with similar experiences.

In addition, the mass shootings get to me. They have become all too common. I was traveling to North Carolina for a wedding when I met the grandparents of one of the little girls who was killed in the Sandy Hook Elementary School shooting. I could feel their sadness and devastation. They told me about her and how much they missed her.

The shootings inside the Charleston church really affected me, too. I grew up in South Carolina and that national news story was in my "backyard." I interviewed the families and saw them in court forgiving and opening their hearts to the man who was responsible. I wondered if he knew how generations would be affected by his evil acts. I thought about the men and women who could tell he was "lost" and welcomed him into their Bible study. He took their lives while they were trying to save his.

Now that I am a mother, the tears flow so much easier when I report these stories. I think of my daughter in any and every situation and pray for God to always protect her. The stories constantly remind me to pray for our country and our leaders. I want good to overcome evil and pray for God's mercy, peace, and wisdom.

Another memorable news story that hit me hard was the death of Roger Ailes, Fox News Channel's former CEO. The news broke during one of my segments on *Fox & Friends* on the morning of May 18, 2017. I was in the middle of interviewing one of my closest friends, Laurie, who had overcome breast cancer, married her surgeon, had a miracle baby, and started a thriving business. We allotted her and her husband time on the show to tell their story but had to cut it short when the news broke of Roger's death at the age of seventy-seven. The news came less than a year after Roger resigned from Fox News in disgrace. Numbers 32:23 says, "You may be sure that your sin will find you out." This was true of Roger Ailes. His secrets found him out and cost him everything he'd built.

And now he was dead.

The report that came across the wire said he died from a sub-dural hematoma, a complication of a head injury he suffered in a fall in his home. I couldn't help but think how different this news would have been received by the nation if it had not been preceded by the moral fall that truly took his life. The man was a giant in our industry even before he launched Fox News. He started out at the bottom and worked his way up. A native of Ohio, he never lost touch with the workingman mentality. In the 1960s he started out as a production assistant on *The Mike Douglas Show* then worked his way up to producer. In 1968, at the young age of twenty-eight, he served as Richard Nixon's media adviser, helping him win the presidency. In 1984 he worked on Ronald Reagan's reelection campaign, then helped put Reagan's vice president, George H. W. Bush, in the White House in 1988. Five years later he turned around CNBC, then launched a second cable channel he called America's Talking. It later became MSNBC.

Roger Ailes's name appears throughout this book because he changed my life. He gave me my chance on the national level and believed in me as I moved up the ranks at Fox News. When I had the chance at my dream job, Roger had the final say. He entrusted a spot on *Fox & Friends* to me. He did more than give me this opportunity. He was a mentor who helped me become the professional I am today. Roger used to say that negative people make positive people sick. I took these words to heart. The man changed America with Fox News and he changed me as well.

Although the news of his death left me in shock I had a job to do. I looked into the camera and reported the news. His death became our show that day. Toward the end of it Steve, Brian, and I sat on the couch with Geraldo Rivera. He was a good friend of Roger's and has been with Fox News for nearly fifteen years. We all did as Roger encouraged us to do—speak our minds. It was tough because we wanted to respect the feelings of the women accusers who worked with us and still remember the man who helped catapult our careers. We were torn. Before I spoke, I prayed and asked God for the words to say. God answered my prayer. I paid tribute to Roger for starting the Fox News Channel. He gave me a chance to live my dream, be a good mother, and provide for my family. As I signed off the air at 8:59 A.M. I said something like this: "We all have fallen short and sinned. Roger paid the ultimate price for his. Rest in Peace, Mr. Ailes."

We all sat there in silence after the show. Our staff came out on set and we all had so many questions. The building was quiet. We were all in shock. We truly celebrated the great memories we had of him, yet hanging over the moment was the darkness that had been revealed just one year earlier.

Then the tears came. I went up to my office and other anchors poured in and we just hugged each other and cried. Throughout the day I appeared on other Fox News shows and talked about Roger. I don't know that I will ever fully get over this tragic story. This one was particularly personal and sad on so many levels. I still pray for his wife and son. I pray that others will learn from his life, both the good and the bad.

Roger's fall reminds me of how fragile life is—not just our physical existence, but our integrity and reputation. I know many people mocked Vice President Pence when he made it public that he never goes out to eat or to a place where alcohol is served alone with a member of the opposite sex. Nor does he allow himself to be alone in a room with any woman except his wife. He does this not because he thinks a woman might make a pass at him or that he might be tempted to make a pass at her. He does it to put walls around his integrity, to guard himself against the very appearance of evil.

The vice president knows what Roger Ailes and many others have learned the hard way. At the end of our lives all that really matters is our character and the way we've treated other people. When I stand before the Lord someday, He will not care about the ratings of any of the news shows I've anchored or how many history makers I've interviewed. All that will matter is whether or not I loved Him, loved His children, and let His light shine through me. That is the life I want to pursue. I pray it is the life you have discovered through these pages.

# What's Next?

Do not say, "Why were the old days better than these?"
For it is not wise to ask such questions.

—ECCLESIASTES 7:10

WHEN I FIRST started working on this book I couldn't help but ask myself why I was writing it. My life didn't seem that interesting to me. But then it hit me: this isn't really my story. My prayer is that what you've just read is really just my story of what God has done in me, through me, and for me. Every good thing I've accomplished, every positive impact I may have left on other people, all the honor and glory goes to God, not me. He has been so good to me, beginning with the amazing family He allowed me to be born into. I really took His goodness and grace for granted until that snowy day at the cabin in the mountains when He saved me. Since then I try not to let a day go by without reminding myself that I've lived a blessed life and thanking God for it.

The amazing thing about this life God has given me is that I know He's far from finished. I do not know how many days He will give me on this earth, but I know I want to use them all for Him. What might that look like? Only God knows. I do not know what He might have in store for me. I love the job with which He has blessed me. If God so chooses, I would stay at Fox News forever. I cannot think of a better place to live out the professional calling God has on my life, or a better audience with which to share it.

Yet my job is only one small part of the life God has given me. In 2015 He blessed me with my precious daughter, Hayden. I cannot wait to see where God takes us on our journey as a mom and daughter. Hayden has already taught me so much about life. God may well bless me with other children, possibly even through adoption. I do not know. Whether He does or does not, my prayer is that someday my child or my children will love God because of the example I set for her or them.

I know the journey ahead of me will not be easy. Life never is. God has carried me through many difficulties and heartbreaks in the past, and I know He will in the future. When I walked through the Valley of the Shadow of Death as I said good-bye to my grandparents and to my baby (which God took home before I ever got to meet her), my Lord was there with me. In John 16:33 Jesus reminded us that in this world we would have trouble. He didn't say that we might have trouble, or that troubles would only hit those with whom God is disappointed. All of God's children will have trouble in this fallen world. But then Jesus gave one of the most precious promises in all the Bible: "But take heart! I have overcome the world." That's the promise that allows me to go forward into an uncertain future. Through good days and bad, through times of blessing and times of heartache, I will always take heart because the One who loves me so much that He gave His life for me has overcome the world. What is next for me? I do not know. But whatever may come I know I will not face it alone because my God will never leave me or forsake me. That promise isn't just for me. It is for everyone who will love Him back just as He loves us. We can all have hope because God's love will never let us down.

# The Unexpected Journey

When times are good, be happy; but when times are
bad, consider this: God has made the one as well as the
other. Therefore, no one can discover anything about
their future.

—ECCLESIASTES 7:14

TWO YEARS AGO, as I put the finishing touches on the book
you have just read, I wrote:

What is next for me? I do not know. But whatever may
come I know I will not face it alone because my God
will never leave me or forsake me. That promise isn't
just for me. It is for everyone who will love Him back
just as He loves us. We can all have hope because God's
love will never let us down.

Six months after this book first came out, those words were
put to the test like never before in my life when my marriage to
Will ended. Divorce is so intensely painful and personal and these
matters are private ones, but I will say Will and I wish each other
the best and we will remain friends. We are grateful to have a
beautiful daughter together and she is our top priority.

For me, there have been several really bad days at different
stages in my life. There was one experience that really tested me.
In fact, I was wishing the last trumpet would sound and Jesus
would come riding down from heaven and take us all home. I
wasn't suicidal. I was just tired of all the sadness and the darkness
of those days and ready to be home with Jesus. I longed for heaven
and the end of suffering, pain, and tears.

I called two of my friends in my Bible study and asked them to pray for me. One of them called to pray with me over the phone. In our conversation she said something that didn't resonate with me at first. I called her back to ask her about what she had said and she repeated the message, "Ainsley, do not fight with the same swords or you will lose the battle."

To say I prayed about this doesn't tell the full story. I didn't just pray. I cried out to God. My reputation as a Christian was under attack. I faced a very uncertain future and I was simply broken, broken before God. I went into my room and shut out the world.

I blared praise and worship music, sat down on my bed, and started pouring out my heart to God. Because I found myself in this particular battle in which I did not know how to fight, I also opened my Bible to Ephesians 6:10–17 that begins, "Finally, be strong in the Lord and in his mighty power. Put on the full armor of God, so that you can take your stand against the devil's schemes. For our struggle is not against flesh and blood, but against . . . the spiritual forces of evil in the heavenly realms." If ever a verse described the battle in which I now found myself, this was it.

Lauren Daigle's song "Rescue" began to play. A friend from South Carolina sent me this beautiful Christian song. She insisted I hear the lyrics. From the time I first heard it, I kept listening to it over and over. The song is powerful, but on this night when I had reached the end of my strength, the song spoke to me with power. The lyrics reassured me that God had heard my cry and he was sending out his army into the darkest of nights to rescue me. As the song played, I saw in my mind an image of white stallions running toward me as fast as their legs could carry them, their manes blowing in the wind. On their backs I saw the angels of heaven, dressed in the armor of God, coming to fight my battles for me. I felt myself surrounded by their presence, protected from any attacks Satan wanted to throw at me. In the midst of it all I felt the reassurance from God that He was going to rescue me. Tears flowed again, a mixture of relief and joy and sadness all rolled into one.

When I awoke the next day, I cried out to God, praising Him for His presence. My friend had told me not to fight with the same swords with which I found myself under attack. She was right. I didn't need to. I was certain God was going to take care of me. I did not know how any of this was going to turn out. God had this. *This is your battle, God, not mine*, I prayed. *I'm giving this all to you.*

The next weekend, a friend invited me to her house in Connecticut. I needed to get out of the city and get away from everything and be surrounded by peace. On Sunday, I told my friend I needed to go to church. There was a Hillsong satellite church nearby (I visit the Hillsong church in New York City occasionally and love the music), so my friend, her son, and I went. I found a seat in the front row of the balcony. At the beginning of the service there were so many distractions, but I knew in my spirit that I needed to be there. Soon I discovered why. The lights dimmed. A young woman walked out on stage and started singing Lauren Daigle's song "Rescue." As she sang, projected on the screen behind her was an image of a white stallion running, its mane blowing in the wind just like the stallions I saw in my mind's eye when I poured out my heart to God at my lowest moment. "Thank you, God," I whispered in prayer. Now I knew why I needed to be at that church on that morning. Through this song and video, God was gently whispering, *I've got this, Ainsley. Don't worry.* And He carried me through.

That is the main message I want you to hear. Changes take place in all our lives, and I have been through a few since the hardcover version of this book was first released. No matter what you may go through, God will be there. He loves you and He will take care of you. I am no one special, as I have said many times in this book. I'm just a girl from South Carolina that has witnessed God work in her life in amazing ways from the time I was a little girl.

More than a year has passed since that morning at the Hillsong church and in that time I have discovered that it's easiest to see God at work when we are at our lowest. As for the judgements, I cannot change perceptions of me. All I can say is in the midst of the storm, God did not abandon me.

God didn't just carry me through the dark days of my life. He also gave me hope by healing my heart and opening my eyes to look ahead, not behind. Over and over He reminded me that I have a great life even though it's different than what I expected.

Needless to say, I am happy. God heals my wounds and makes me whole.

I love Jesus. I want to be in His will. And I love my child. Gosh, I love being a mom. I wanted Hayden so badly and God heard my prayer. He shows Himself to me through her little personality. She loves Him and we pray daily. She says a blessing before each meal, goes to Vacation Bible School in the summer, sings in our church choir, and regularly talks about God, Jesus, and heaven when we read a Christian book every night. She asks a lot of questions and I try to answer them in the best, Biblical way. When I am teaching her lessons, I try to reprimand her in a Godly way, reminding her how God wants us to treat each other.

I have learned that we all face hurt, but what makes us men and women of character is how we face the pain. We have a choice. We can either hold on to that hurt and let it continue to consume us, or we can release it to God. I found the only way to heal is to give it to God. Let go and let God. I have to forgive in order to be the best Ainsley.

What's next for me? I asked that question before in the epilogue to this book. At the time I wrote that I saw the storm clouds on the horizon which shaped how the book ended. Today I find myself in a different place. I finally feel like myself again. I once again have genuine excitement about the future even though I have no idea what that future may look like. Here's what gave me hope.

First, I know who I am as a child of God. Going through traumatic experiences can leave a person second-guessing decisions they've made. But, I know "whose" I am. I am God's child. I know my worth. I am a child of the King and I am confident in that.

When many go through tough situations they find themselves questioning their self-worth. If you are in that position, I want to encourage you by reassuring you that you are beloved by God, that you matter to Him, and He wants His best for you. That's the assurance you have as a child of God. For me, I know I am His. I know He made me special and with a purpose. How do I know this? The Bible says that's God's plan for all His children, not just me. You are loved beyond measure. That is why we can face the future with hope.

I have also been blessed with the perfect job for my circumstances. For the past five years I have had the privilege of anchoring a morning show where the bulk of my workday is finished before my daughter even wakes up. I don't mind getting up at 3 a.m. every day if it means I can pick her up from school and then spend my afternoons with her.

She's my little partner in life. I am able to go with her to her various classes and activities. I know very few full-time working parents get this privilege so I never take it for granted. My cup runneth over.

Friends have asked if I will ever get married again. Honestly, I have no idea. That's in God's hands, not mine. I know I am open to the idea. However, if that turns out not to be God's plan for my life, I'm okay with that. I still have a lot of love and fulfillment in my life. I have my God, my daughter, my family, and my friends. I have a job at Fox News and I am extremely happy. I also know, although I am single, I am not broken. My life is not somehow empty because I am making my way through life without a partner, but I am complete in Christ. I can honestly say that whatever He has planned for me, I'm ready. I want the light He has placed within me to shine bright wherever He leads me.

# Acknowledgments

THANK YOU, LORD, for loving me first.

MY DEAREST HAYDEN, you are the gift your father and I prayed for and God blessed us with the one who is best for us: YOU. I have loved you since before you were born and I will love you well beyond my dying day. You are so smart, funny, and beautiful. You are innocent, honest, and good. My life's mission is to serve Christ and be your mother. Proverbs 31:30 tells us "Charm is deceptive, and beauty is fleeting; but a woman who fears the Lord is to be praised." Your character counts and beauty comes from your heart. Hayden, you have just one life. Make it matter, my precious child.

TO WILL, THANK you for teaching me to value life. Our wedding weekend was wonderful, but nothing will ever compare to the weekend of fulfillment we experienced on Friday, November 6, 2015. When you handed me our daughter, Hayden DuBose Proctor, my life changed for the better. Thank you for your support, memories, and joy. You have given me wonderful gifts, but my favorite will forever be motherhood.

THANK YOU TO my family. I am so blessed to have each of you in my life. We have mostly had the best of times, but even in my worst of times . . . I had you holding me up. Your love, loyalty, and support have never wavered and I thank God for putting us together. I know He has placed me in a unique position, but that doesn't make my job more important than yours. We each have different roles, but we are a team bonded together by blood and nothing will ever tear us apart.

THANK YOU TO Fox News executives and coworkers for allowing me to be myself, for being my New York family, for giving me a chance and a platform to change lives and our country for the better.

RUPERT MURDOCH, THANK you for starting the Fox News Channel, making all my dreams come true, and giving me a chance. I am forever grateful.

Suzanne Scott, you have been there for me through my life's major ups and downs, all of them happening in New York—the city where God shaped me the most. You're a beautiful mother, strong leader, and compassionate friend.

DIANNE BRANDI, THANK you for being so generous to me and always looking out for my best interests.

SEAN HANNITY, THANK you for launching my career and being my mentor.

Lauren Petterson and Gavin Hadden—you are the beautiful brains behind *Fox & Friends*—always letting us get the credit, when you deserve the recognition. There's an old saying for a producer, "Know your anchors." Thank you for knowing our passions and allowing us to be ourselves on air. Your jobs never end and go well beyond delivering the news. You make an indelible difference in my life, in Steve's and Brian's, and in the millions who wake up to *Fox & Friends* every morning. They choose us because of you!

To my coanchors, Brian Kilmeade and Steve Doocy: thank you

for teaching me so much on a daily basis, always having my back, and not taking life too seriously. I can honestly say, waking up at three A.M. is never a dread because each day is fun and exciting!

LIZ NAIFEH, YOU are so special. Fox News made you my assistant, but God made you my "sister." Your precious mother took her last breath when you were just a baby. I can't imagine her grief as she suffered her sickness and had to say goodbye to three little ones. But she married a good man and he did an outstanding job! I know you'll be reunited with your mom again and she will tell you, just as God will, "Well done!"

MARK TABB, I thank you from the bottom of my heart for your valiant efforts in making this book come together. I knew from the beginning you were the one I was supposed to choose to help me write *The Light Within Me*. Thank you for being a good example and dedicating everything you do to the Lord. Thank you for being so cooperative and helping me condense the pages of my life into nineteen chapters.

TO THE HARPERCOLLINS team, thank you, thank you, thank you, for giving me the opportunity to share my faith in these pages. I truly believe God is using all of us to share His love.

Thank you Brian Murray, Jonathan Burnham, Tina Andreadis, Rachel Elinsky, Alieza Schwimer, and Stephanie Cooper.

Matt Harper and Lisa Sharkey, I won't ever be able to thank you enough. Your compassion and understanding throughout this process is most appreciated.

THANK YOU, OLIVIA Metzger, for believing in me and never underestimating me. You are a good friend, mother, and agent!

# Acknowledgments

To Cait Hoyt for giving me a new title—author. My parents' words of wisdom and God's mighty works have been shared because of you. Thank you for putting their advice in bookstores, homes, and hands all around the world.

To New York, thank you for teaching me how to dream.

To Paris, thank you for teaching me how to live.

# About the Author

AINSLEY EARHARDT is the author of the bestselling children's books *Take Heart, My Child* and *Through Your Eyes*, and is one of the cohosts of the number one cable morning news show, *Fox & Friends*, on the Fox News Channel. She has been a correspondent for Sean Hannity's show, *Hannity*; a cohost of *Fox & Friends First*; an anchor for *Fox & Friends Weekend*; a host of Fox's *All-American New Year's Eve, America's News Headquarters, Outnumbered*, and *The Five*. She has also been a panelist on *The Live Desk* and has appeared with Neil Cavuto and Tucker Carlson on their shows. She lives in New York City.